The Universal Cockroach

Copyright © 2006 Nawfal Moughnieh
All rights reserved.
ISBN: 1-4196-3180-2
Library of Congress Control Number : 2006903218

To order additional copies, please contact us.
BookSurge, LLC
www.booksurge.com
1-866-308-6235
orders@booksurge.com

NAWFAL
MOUGHNIEH

THE UNIVERSAL COCKROACH
A World Vision

2006

The Universal Cockroach

TABLE OF CONTENTS

The Universal Cockroach	1
I Was Once Great	11
Common Ground	13
Global Romanticism and Rationalism	19
Theory and Vision	25
Survival of the Fittest	29
The Power Of Science	31
Strength In Unity	35
What's In It For The STRONG?	37
What's In It For Us?	39
Let Us Imagine	45
Global Security	51
Equal Global Opportunity	57
Too Many	59
On The Road	61
The Greatest Obstacle	65
National And Cultural Tolerance	67
How To Go From A To B?	69
Am I Naïve?	73
Who Gets What?	75
Nation State Inefficiencies	77
The Trojan Horse	81
Education Versus Specialization	85
Basic Lessons	89
Problems In Heaven	93
Balance Of Power	95

Is It Too Late?	101
The Consequence Of The Status Quo	105
Transitory Period	107
Can I Go Anywhere?	111
Cultural Integration	113
Nationalism And Democracy	117
What Is The National Interest?	121
Good For You And For Me	123
World Population	125
Philanthropy And Self Interest	127
Energy	129
Religion	131
Global versus Regional and Local Governments	133
Economics	135
The Most Important Foundation For Democracy	143
What A Global Government Cannot Do?	145
Global Nation Constitution	147
A Final Thought	149
References	151

ACKNOWLEDGMENTS

I'd like to thank all the people in this world with whom I interacted, all the cultures that I have been exposed to. Special thanks to my original editor, Pascal Sakr Kassis, whose editorial suggestions showed remarkable sensitivity and depth of knowledge. Thanks to my ever professional editor, Debbie Lovatt, for her ability to edit my book and yet retain my style, and last but not least thanks to my part time employee Fouad Mezher for his art work.

To My Late Father

THE UNIVERSAL COCKROACH

This essay is foremost a mental journey. I have always enjoyed mental trips.

I would like to thank my late Father for telling me to go and find the answer myself whenever I asked him a philosophical question as a curious young man. He refused to shackle my brain with preconceived ideas and gave me the freedom to think. My Mother has given me love and balance, and my brother and two sisters have taught me to compromise.

Back in 1988 when I was studying for my MBA in Rhode Island in the United States, I was watching an interview on television with a person who was talking about a man who wanted to commit suicide by jumping from a bridge and who had been prevented from doing so by a passerby. The talker was highlighting that the passerby ran to help without much thought—his intuitive response said something about all of us being united in this Universe.

A few days after watching that show it dawned on me that all of us are one: me, you, the chair, earth, everything. Don't ask me how I reached this conclusion—if it can be labeled a conclusion in the first place—because it just popped up. The important point is that inside of me there is a desire to unite.

I'm not sure if this is natural. It might go back to the period when the child is in its mother's womb, its awareness of the outside world is negligible if not nil, and thus at that stage its sense of security might be utmost compared to the whole period of its life. Maybe we all long for this sense of security and warmth—or maybe state of unconsciousness—which we might incidentally achieve when we die, depending on one's beliefs about what happens after death.

A few years later, around 1993, I was in San Francisco watching Bill Clinton on TV in one of his presidential debates. He was talking about how the American people should not be divided between "us" and "them," how "they" all should be "us."

I started wondering whether he would have said that if he did not think that it was the right message to convey, or if it had not had a broad acceptance within the American people. Of course I noticed that he did not include the whole world when using the word "us." He still divided the world into "us," meaning the United States, and "them," the rest of the world. It was implicit in his speech.

Needless to say he was running for the presidency of the United States, and his constituents were American citizens and not citizens of other countries. The way he divided the world into "us "and "them" was understandable, politically wise, in order to reach his goals, but definitely not visionary. His speech gave me a sense of relief, as I realized that I was not the sole man wanting to unite, but that entire societies did as well, even though the difference remained on a national versus global level.

THE UNIVERSAL COCKROACH

A few years later, while working for a company in Saudi Arabia, I had a lot of free time and spent it reading. I read political science books and books about the history of the world. One that I greatly enjoyed was *The Structure of Scientific Revolutions*, by Thomas S. Kuhn. The back cover commentary written by N.W. said, "...Science is not the steady, cumulative acquisitions of knowledge that is portrayed in textbooks. Rather, it is a series of peaceful interludes punctuated by intellectually violent revolutions...in each of which one conceptual world is replaced by another."

This book has enhanced my sense of always standing on shaky ground intellectually. It is a healthy position because always being conscious of the non-absolute status of your position on any subject makes you less polarized towards others who do not share your opinion, culture, or way of thinking.

This concept that places truth on shaky grounds is not new to the intellectual history of humankind; Emmanuel Kant, the nineteenth century philosopher, clearly stated the active role of the mind in comprehending the outside world. Thus reality is unable to be perceived as is; the mind plays an act in constructing it.

Any student of Western philosophy knows that attempts by twentieth century philosophers to give a firm ground to reality has only resulted in changing the definition of the problem. As W.T. Jones in his series *A History of Western Philosophy* stated when he was talking about the place of Wittgenstein in twentieth century philosophy: "It is not philosophy slipped back into the Kantian form of constructivism; it is rather that the problem of the relation of mind to its objects has been replaced by the problem of the relation of language to the world."

It is possible that in the twenty-first century the problem will be replaced by another.

While I am acutely aware that it is impossible for me to reach a state of philosophical bliss, I feel I can contribute in some small way to the future of mankind by providing a futuristic vision. However, before this is done it seems to me it is important to put the history of mankind into some perspective, while acknowledging in advance that it is not the only plausible perspective.

Due to the lack of communication between civilizations, all mankind has lived in different civilizations, and as time and technology progressed, each civilization became aware of the existence of others, the first reaction often being one of caution. Each civilization tried to destroy or dominate the other, resulting in great wars. As the level of communication became more intense, each civilization adopted foreign views and ultimately considered them as its own. What used to be transferred through bloodshed, henceforth is transferred by communication. The trend is far from over.

Humankind has finished the first phase of its history. We might call that phase "The phase of independent development." The second phase, the one we are still going through, we will call "The phase of awareness, domination and integration." In the future the human race needs to work to reach the third phase, "The phase of global development."

THE UNIVERSAL COCKROACH

In the first phase, the seeds of conflict and enrichment were planted. The world has been enriched tremendously through the development of all independent cultures. However, when civilizations came in contact with each other, often conflict arose. Sometimes this contact between different civilizations resulted in integration, sometimes in domination, but at all times an exchange of ideas took place, and this exchange is the basis of the creation of the third phase.

While development is a continuous process in all three phases, it is not evenly distributed in the first two phases. I have called the third phase as such, because development will be even for all humankind. However, the philosophical, cultural, and technological foundations will need to be developed before entering upon the third phase, where humankind and all living creatures on earth will reap the benefits.

This perspective, which bears in itself wishful thinking concerning the progressive nature of the history of mankind, can be thought of as an objective. A question can be asked about what needs to be done in order for the future of mankind to be better than its past.

The objective of this essay is to assist our passage through the second phase with the least damage possible to humankind, and to try to lay the foundation for the third phase.

It would be safe to assume that the most modern person living today has at least part of his thinking based on principles developed in Ancient Greece, or even the ancient Middle East. One can argue whether the effect of one civilization was greater than the other, but there is no question of the effect of past civilizations on each other, and on the way we think today. We should not reject the present, but use it to have a better future. When this work evokes changing our political system from one of multiple nations to a system of global government, it should not be thought of as a rejection of the present system, because whatever system we are in, it is still a boat that we board to sail the seas, rough and calm. The intention is to build a new boat that will weather out the rough seas ahead in a far better way than our present vessel. The main difference is while each country is sailing a different boat, some of which will sink or suffer extensive damage, we will try to put the human race in one boat that will bring them safely to shore.

Needless to say, the new boat has to be well thought out, or else it and the human race will sink.

Lord Falkland said, "When it is not necessary to change, it is necessary not to change." This statement is very true, still what is not necessary to change is not clear; if we are living in a system that is producing a mixture of desirable and undesirable results, such as our system of multiple nations, how could we know if changing to a new system is necessary, or whether it is only necessary to change some elements of the existing one, or if the existing system has in itself the ability to change incrementally with the least amount of disturbance.

Looking at our existing system, one can safely say that development is not even in all countries. Some countries are on the brink of disaster or already experiencing it, as is the case in some African countries. Without going into detail as to whether this is the result of external or internal factors, or a combination of both, not only is there no effective international mechanism capable of alleviating the suffering of human beings on a global basis whenever needed, there will never be one as long as we are living in a system of multiple nations.

The weakness of our system of multiple nations is that it divides the world into "us" and "them." This division will not be overcome as long as the human race lives in a world divided into countries.

Back to our main question: How can we know whether it is necessary to change or not? The answer is very simple: We cannot. But how can we conceptualize change, and figure out when it is necessary to change, when we do not even know why an apple falls to the ground? Newton and Einstein attempted to explain just that, with little success. It seems to me the answer lies somewhere else, but where?

Looking at the history of mankind, we find people believed in God without any physical proof of His existence. This fact gives me encouragement, because in order for our global state to exist, people need to believe in it, but we are unable to give any proof to humankind that the new system will be better than the existing one, so we are left asking humankind to have faith in what we are saying, but is that enough? Of course not.

Many religions and ideologies have used force to expand. Wouldn't it be justified for us to use force for our vision to be realized? The answer is no. First, even with the use of force, religions were unable to encompass everyone under their faith, and second, each religion claimed the rightness of its path and the falseness of others, thus it had elements of unity as well as division. No matter what level of force is used, there will always be a counter force. Have we failed in our history to unite? I like to think we did not entirely.

A future society, to be inclusive, has to allow difference in perspective, and not only that. The future mind has to consider fellow human beings as us, irrespective of anything and everything.

That is easier said than done. People tend to think about each other in terms of what differentiates them more than what unites them.

What about scarcity of resources? Even if all human beings achieve a level where all will think that they belong to the same community, the very practical problem of feeding everyone will remain, let alone speaking about who gets what. Wouldn't this lead us back to a survival of the fittest situation?

Until now we have been acting freely in many ways. People can eat as much as and whatever they want, they can have as many children as they want, and can drive their car for as long as they want. It sounds like these are the properties of affluent societies, but wouldn't it be safe to say that this is only possible if other societies do not benefit from that affluence, due to the limited nature of resources? Again back to survival of the fittest situation. It seems the more we think of the matter, the more we realize that while some of us will enjoy life, many of us will not; it seems as if it is the natural way of life.

I have to confess that as I am inclined towards a new system this thought depresses me. I cannot lie to myself and say it is more than a vision. The Communist Manifesto is on my mind.

What I mean to say is that Communism is as good a theory as any other. One can argue about its strong or weak points, but I do not think that anyone could assert that it is not a theory. However, the vision has problems when applied. It seems to me that a well-built theory does not guarantee or nullify the possibility of the survival of the vision behind it. A theory is kind of a sophisticated marketing tool for the vision.

There is no need for a theory to market our vision of global government. The vision will have to survive or perish without one.

The task is now changed from creating and proving a theory, to formulating a vision and trying to market this vision without claiming its absolute righteousness, not because the new vision is not right, but because of the impossible attainability of absolute truth, at least from a philosophical point of view.

What a difficult situation I have put myself in! Here I am basically saying as the Greek philosopher used to say: "I know that I do not know," and what is more, I am also saying that absolute knowledge is impossible to attain; thus, since no one holds the absolute truth, we are left with each other. Therefore, the only possibility remaining is to get closer to each other as a human race, or else all of us will suffer.

I realize that I have not only put myself in a difficult situation, I have put everyone who wants to prove anything in the same situation. To move in any direction a route that differs from that of science and logic needs to be taken.

Today I stood beneath a big tree and thought that through touching the tree I might make it feel better. I touched it but I don't know if it felt better. I wondered if this tree knows something I don't, or whether it knows that there are a few birds on its branches. And a pleasant thought came to my mind: This tree is harmless; it is all benefits. Another thought came to my mind: We are living in a world of miracles. I wish we all were Alice in Wonderland. I am content with being Alice, but wouldn't it be better to be Alexander the Great? I do not think so, but this is only my opinion.

Each one of us has become familiar with the world we are living in. Science has deluded us into thinking we understand this world and theories have been built to explain the past and predict the future, but where exactly are we? We are nowhere and everywhere. If knowledge can arguably be attained, then we are at the beginning of a very long trip. Here we are under the certainty that our age is the age of science, proud of ourselves for what we have achieved, giving ourselves the right to be differentiated from fellow human beings because we know more. But what do we know?

Until we have compassion we are predators: the strong for abusing the weak, the weak for trying to abuse the strong whenever the chance arises.

Are we able to see ourselves for what we really are? Can we change the world?

I WAS ONCE GREAT

Where is the Roman Empire and its might? Where is the Hapsburg Empire? Where is Great Britain and her colonies? Time's passage teaches one to be humble.

Today various countries claim to be number one, some claim to be number one in military power, some in technology, some in business, some in all these areas, but none claims to be number one in humility.

Why it is necessary to feel and be humble? Isn't it a function of culture and not a universal virtue? Are there any universal virtues to start with?

There has to be some common ground that the majority of humankind agrees on, or else a global system cannot take off.

COMMON GROUND

One does not have to be a genius to note that the moral message in all religions was directed towards the human being on this planet. It is not my intention to talk about the origin of morals, or whether it can exist in a non-religious society. What is important for me to know is at what stage morals breakdown in our existing system of multiple nations, and what the consequences of such a break down are, if any; then, whether in a system of global government such a breakdown is avoidable, and what benefits human beings would reap from such avoidance.

In our system of multiple nations, morality stops at the door of each country. The universal application of morality cannot be exercised because danger is perceived to come from other groups. Thus, a survival of the fittest strategy is actually applied by each group towards another, with no regard to morals, because morals are perceived as a constraint towards using immoral tools when engaging with other groups in order to survive. Such a strategy is elegantly labeled in political science books as the realist view, where the interests of the state are above all, and a state is allowed to do anything to preserve its national interest.

Thus, in our system of multiple nations it is meaningless to talk about the morality of human beings. It simply does not exist. One can only talk about morality inside a group, the largest group being a country or a union of countries.

To start with, for each person living on this earth and loving his country, his national feeling is the other side of the coin of his biased feelings towards citizens of other countries. Being nationalistic automatically makes one biased. When one divides the world into us and them one is being biased, whether this division is between white and black, or between educated and non-educated or between the citizens of this country and those of another.

This human being is a hypocrite of the first degree, saying one thing and doing the opposite, declaring his or her belief in the universality of morals, and then forgetting about his morals and often acting immorally towards fellow human beings from other countries.

Such behavior of the human beings in our system of multiple nations is partly a consequence of the system of multiple nations, and partly due to the effect of the historical conditions the human being has lived through.

Let's explain that concept in a simple way: in nature we find animals that have wings but have lost their ability to fly. Looking at the historical development of the environment of such animals, we find out that their wings did not suddenly vanish when their environment changed and made them obsolete, but rather that the size, ability, or usage of the wings slowly decreased, until in some animals they vanished completely. More important than a change in the environment leading to physical changes in animals or human beings is the change in behavior in both, and the change in ideas and principles as far as human beings are concerned.

The human beings' historical environment led them to form groups to fulfill their needs for safety and food. In our present times human beings still feel the need to belong to a group to fulfill their needs, but in our modern world not enough thought has gone into the negative consequences of living in a group smaller than the human species.

Our system of multiple nations has affected human beings' behavior, and even if it were suddenly replaced, the behavior and set of ideas developed in the old system would not be changed suddenly or without conflict with the new ideas. Such a conflict can be seen between globalization and nationalism. Globalization today is based on opening markets for technology-producing countries and it is not yet based on a vision of the universality and fellowship of human beings.

This is where we see the value of education to properly develop the required set of ideas and behavior in order for human beings to live in a global nation and rid themselves of attitudes and ideas that are mainly the result of living in the first and second phase.

Long before mankind lived in nations, it went through what we called the first phase, where independent civilizations grew. Few civilizations if any had an equitable law—there were always two laws: one for the rulers and one for the ruled.

The same pattern repeated itself in the second phase: Civilizations that are basically without equitable law came into contact with each other and the blind continued leading the blind. Even now, where people live in multiple nations that have equitable laws, there is no global equitable law for mankind, thus in a system of multiple nations like ours morality for mankind is difficult to be achieved.

It may not be bad after all to be polarized and hypocritical if it maximizes one's chances of survival. The problem with such a position is the impossibility of dividing the human psyche. In plain English, what goes around comes around. If one acts humanely towards one's group and inhumanely towards other groups, then there is an increased tendency for this inhumane mentality to reverse its direction.

Thus, being simultaneously moralistic and immoral is a risky strategy. It might even ensure the extinction rather than the survivability of the human race as a whole, regardless of whether it's the weak or the strong using this strategy.

In a system of global government where all human beings are under the same law, and each person considers herself or himself as "us," morality has a meaning that does not contradict mankind's religious heritage (i.e. The message of universal morality is a hostage in our system of multiple nations—the universal moral message of mankind's religious heritage has been stopped at the door of each country). We are all hypocrites, polarized and biased and will remain such until we live in a world with one entity, until we all become "us."

Here I am introducing morals as the underlying competitive advantage that is necessary but not sufficient to maximize my objective—the welfare of the human race as a whole. I believe that being moral involves thinking and acting at the level of the human race as a whole; one cannot only be concerned with his or her own group and consider oneself to be moral.

What is morality then? Nietzsche considers that morality lies not in kindness but in strength: "Not mankind, but superman is the goal." For Nietzsche mankind does not exist; it is an abstraction.

One needs to be very careful then in defining morality. To start with, nature has made humans dominant over all earth's creatures. However, this does not mean that the human being is superior on all fronts. It is unclear whether the human race will be the one to ultimately survive the test of time. Thus, strength is not well defined in Nietzsche's thought, it is a primitive way of understanding strength. Remember how strong the dinosaurs were? Where are they now? In natural history museums.

Then, how can mankind be moral?

It seems to me a necessary, yet insufficient condition for mankind to achieve morality by having a global equitable law that is enforced globally. This can be best achieved if mankind lives in a system of a global nation.

Here we have a major problem. From a theoretical point of view we are giving all countries a license to get involved in the business of other countries, which is nowadays labeled as interference in the internal affairs of a country.

If we are not careful, strong countries will try to dominate and abuse the weaker ones on the pretext of achieving our vision of globalization, thus the vision of globalization will be a nice tool in the hands of the predators of the world aiming at dominating the whole world, and instead of creating a more humane world we will end up with a global inhumane system.

One has to be careful not to end up with a system worse than the existing one. Following one's romantic feelings alone will not lead to a better world; romance has its place, and cold blooded thinking has to have its place too. The question is: How can we use these two functions in a harmonious and inclusive way? Lucky for us, we are already somewhat successful in doing so.

We find the media in all countries portraying citizens as members of one common family called the nation. This romantic feeling, which is essential to the making of a nation, is in parallel with laws that punish whoever breaks them. Here we see romanticism and rationalism working beautifully to make a nation. This cooperation breaks down at the international level; there we need to create the global romantic citizen, who is at the same time the global rational citizen.

GLOBAL ROMANTICISM AND RATIONALISM

Is there romance in politics? I tend to believe there is romance in all the fabrics of our thought, even the most rational ones.

Is there rationality in politics? I tend to believe there is rationality in all the fabrics of our thoughts, even the most romantic ones.

What is Romance and what is Rationality? I don't exactly know. I have to depend on my intuition to recognize them, knowing that my intuition might be extremely confusing, but I'm not bothered about my confusion because everyone is in a state of confusion.

Such is the human mind: riddles within riddles within riddles. This is why we need compassion.

Today I feel mentally strong, and I am also discouraged. It has been more than a month since I have written anything, I have doubts about everything I have written—not about the central theme of being one global nation, but about how to market this concept, and whether marketing it is good for the long term success of adaptation to this concept by the masses worldwide.

Again, the Communist experience is on my mind. Suppose a wise man told Lenin that Marx's ideas about Communism were advanced, but that applying Communism at that stage of development of humankind would lead to disasters and thus would hurt the long term success of the masses' adaptation to Communism. Suppose the wise man advised Lenin to keep the Communist Manifesto on paper, and let other thinkers improve it and find better ways to implement it.

Could it be that the idea of a global nation is a sound one but that the time has not yet come to apply it?

Let us rephrase the question by asking what the majority of humankind would vote if asked today whether they were in favor of or against a system of globalization? I would say the majority would vote "no."

The question to be asked is what it would take for the majority to vote "yes." I would say more than anything else that humankind would have to think alike on some issues for the vote to be "yes." What are these essential issues?

I have to be honest: I'm still in the process of finding out.

Looking at the European experience, one can say that one of the major reasons for integration was the feeling that if integration did not happen then the powerful state, namely Germany, would walk the way of domination once again. France and Germany were the major forces behind the unification process and others followed—not by force but by conviction.

THE UNIVERSAL COCKROACH

Looking at the world as a whole we see a parallel situation: According to the balance of power principle nations are slowly uniting towards a front that balances the only superpower, the United States.

Indeed, the expansion of the European Union towards Eastern Europe has as much to do with uniting historical Europe as it has to do with creating a superpower that tries to balance the United States. Russia and China are also positioning themselves as counterweights to the American superpower.

Hopefully this balancing act, which is only natural, will continue without bloodshed. If this remains the case, then Russia and China will ultimately join the European Union to create an effective balancing act. At some point the European Union will adopt a new name for itself—it might be called the Global Union. This will happen because the vision will have become unifying the human race, and not only Europeans.

The above paragraphs have to do with global rationalism. Looking at things from a romantic point of view we like to say that the common feeling of brotherhood of humankind will ultimately be the reason for the unification of the world under one nation. My prediction is that during a transitional phase this feeling will not play an important role. However, once the global nation has been established, the ideological basis for unification will very much depend on this feeling. In fact it would be a part of the fellowship not only of humankind but of existence as well.

What I mean by fellowship of existence is the feeling that all of us are somehow in the same boat, and not only humankind or living creatures, but everything including the void. At the level of consciousness there is no difference between living or non-living things, or between material and void, or even between an idea and a thing. As long as the brain is aware of it, it is in the arena of consciousness, even if it is an imaginary idea. (I have allowed myself to be a little imaginary and philosophical; my feet are a little bit above the ground.)

This, I believe, is the romantic ideological basis for the unification of mankind; it is part of the unification of mankind with its external environment.

It might be an attempt for mankind to go back to the mother's womb.

Here I'm trying to romanticize about the future human being. I would imagine this creature to be a baby all its life. A baby because it has overcome all threats to its life, its body does not feel pain anymore because it has devised systems that protect it from any danger. I am not sure how, but somehow the future human being is a baby that is laughing and playing all the time.

Its brain is very simple because it found the answers to all its questions, now it knows which questions are meaningless and which questions are not. It has reached a stage where most questions are meaningless, except those like: "I want to play ball, where are my friends?"

The ultimate objective is to lose consciousness by uniting with the external environment. Death is not an acceptable option. Love is.

THE UNIVERSAL COCKROACH

Is there a place for love in our strategy? I would say yes. I am not sure what love is, as I am not sure of anything else, but I would imagine that feeling love is better than not feeling it. I did not say much, I know; the problem is that saying more makes me more inaccurate.

Enough of imagination...let us get back to the ground. The deterioration of the environment might be the catalyst for unification; this route is a sad one. It is like saying in the 1800s that it would take major world wars for the world to wake up to the horrors of war. It is sad, but true. Well, is there a way for mankind to unite without suffering the consequences of living in a system of multiple nations first? I tend to say no.

Then I ask myself, what is the use of this writing since I have already decided that it will not help prevent catastrophes from happening to mankind as a direct consequence of living in anarchy? Well it is still possible that after these assumed catastrophes humankind will look at this collection of ideas as a general road map towards its survival. Of course this road map is extremely general and full of silly ideas, seen from the perspective of a hundred years from now, but then again it is only natural when the human being tries to better himself.

I once asked myself about the biggest benefit Communism gave to humankind, and I asked myself about the biggest benefit of religion to mankind...I found the answer to be that both Communism and religion have focused the spotlight on the universe. They both took a universal view. I feel the universal view is the right view in looking at everything. Both contained an implicit assumption of unification at the level of consciousness: religion unified the human being with the universe by giving them both one sole creator or multiple creators, and Communism unified humankind with the universe by denying them a creator outside the universe. It seems unification has been an implicit objective all the way through history.

THEORY AND VISION

I have mentioned before that our vision of one global nation does not need a theory to back it up.

The reason for my decision not to develop a theory to back up this vision is primarily that I don't know how to develop one, and also that I don't believe such a theory is beneficial for the long term survival of the vision.

A theory is a marketing tool. Whether the vision is being marketed successfully or not has nothing to do with determining if it is the right or wrong vision to pursue.

Even if we agreed for the sake of argument that a theory is not only a marketing tool but a way to understand and predict some phenomena, then once a theory is developed to back up a vision, we may assume that the one developing the theory is actually implying that since the theory is right, then the vision is right too. Here lies a major threat to the survivability of the vision, because all one has to do to sway people from the vision is to prove the theory wrong, or at least try to cast a shadow of doubt over the implicit or explicit assumptions that every theory has.

I feel I need to give a more solid foundation to the vision of unification. Not in the sense of giving solid proof, but in the sense of saying simply that the choice of unification or anarchy is simply a choice that every human being can make, at least mentally. It is like running to prevent someone from committing suicide by jumping off a bridge; one can look and do nothing, or one can try to do something.

No theory in the world can show what is better to do; it is simply a choice to be a predator or a compassionate person. The job is to show that if one opts to be living in a world of multiple nations, then one has chosen to be a predator, and if one opts to live in a world of one humane global government, then one opts to be a compassionate person.

The methods used to understand and predict the natural sciences are being used to understand and predict the social world. This flaw in thinking is understandable because of the success of these methods in understanding and predicting the physical world. However, it is no secret that all scientific methods have failed, until now, to reach a final understanding of our existing world.

It is not clear what the approaches will be in the future in order to have a deeper understanding. What is clear to me is that we are reaching a point of diminishing returns; no matter how much we use our scientific knowledge, the scientific foundations are not capable of giving us a deeper understanding, and therefore a major breakthrough is needed.

Waiting for this major breakthrough is futile because, unlike the physical world where almost everything happens without our interference or understanding, our social life is largely of our making.

This is my underlying assumption; or else, if everything is predetermined then there is no need to have a vision or to try to steer things in one direction or another.

SURVIVAL OF THE FITTEST

What do Alexander the Great, Julius Caesar, Napoleon, and Hitler have in common? They all had the same dream to unite the world, and all failed to realize it.

Not only was their dream the same, but so was the reason for their failure.

When you say "I am right," you are actually dividing the world into "us" and "them."

When you say "We all have the same rights under the law," you are uniting the world.

Until these two simple facts are fully understood the human being will not achieve peace of mind.

Why is the world divided into so many nations? Part of the answer to me is that the human being is still saying "I am right," which means others are wrong or at least different, thus others are not "us," and the consequence is a world in turmoil; the objective of each group is to destroy, dominate, or coexist with other groups.

After reading Charles Darwin's *The Origin of Species* I was a little bit confused.

My confusion came from wondering what Darwin meant by the word "fittest," when he said that the fittest species would survive, as well as in each species the fittest would survive.

My problem was my inability to define who would be the fittest in any game until the game is played and the results are clear. Thus, although Darwin has correctly described the quality that the winner possess as of now, he did not describe which qualities the winner would possess under which conditions in the future; all he was able to say is that it appeared such and such species had survived under such and such conditions because of such and such attributes. Projection into the future as to who would survive is far more difficult.

Applying such a line of thought to the human species, one can say that it is impossible to know who would survive the power struggle among the different nations that exist today, thus it would be better to have all humans under one global system. It would ensure the survival of all; the social safety net would ensure that all have a minimum level of protection. It's like everybody would have bread and rice to eat but few would have caviar.

THE POWER OF SCIENCE

I feel science and religion are incapable of solving the problems of the human race; they both failed to solve old problems without creating new ones.

On the religious front, the minute a civilization discovered a new religion that gave it power, it started imposing its belief on other civilizations often by using force. This resulted in great miseries in the past.

On the scientific front, no sooner is a technology to ease human life implemented than problems arise from using such a technology.

However, from a conceptual basis, science has power over religion, not because science succeeded where religion failed, but because science never closed the door in the face of new ideas or new ways of explaining things, even if this ultimately means wiping out old theories and replacing them with new ones.

This openness of science to change, and the relative ease of scientists in accepting challenges to their ideas by other scientists in a peaceful manner is not paralleled in the social life of human beings. We rarely, if ever, hear of a scientist who killed another over a difference of opinion. In fact, difference of opinion is considered by the scientific community as the tool with which to reach the truth. At the same time we keep hearing about many countries where people get killed or are persecuted because they have different religious, political or social ideas.

This tolerance of alternative ideas within the scientific community needs to spill over into all aspects of the life of the human being, and needs to be taught to the future human beings too.

Tolerance is not the only lesson that can be learned from the scientific community; another lesson is that the scientific community considers itself global in nature.

The criteria by which someone is considered a member of the scientific community have nothing to do with her or his national origin, religious or political affiliations. No matter what a scientist's beliefs are, it is her or his abilities that grant him membership of this exclusive club; there is very little bias in such a selection.

A scientist would never hesitate to consider the opinions or experiments of his fellow scientists, whoever they are, if those opinions or experiments are scientific in nature.

The fact that all scientists are studying a universal theme which is nature in all its living and non-living forms makes their criteria for membership of their club independent of the common bias that we see in our social and political world. There is an implicit assumption within the scientific community that a good human brain can be found anywhere in this world.

THE UNIVERSAL COCKROACH

Since we are all human beings, the criteria for our belonging to the same club are already there. However, the same arrogance that made human beings think in the past that earth is the center of the universe, makes them believe that some deserve to dominate others because they have more money, or are more educated, or they belong to a more powerful country, or they claim the righteousness of some religion or philosophy.

STRENGTH IN UNITY

One of the major divisions that needs to be eliminated in order to have a better world is our system of multiple nations; the fact that human beings live in different countries means that we are divided into groups. Each differentiates itself from the others; we will automatically have divergence of interest. Needless to say, citizens of the same country have divergence of interests too. However, such a divergence of interests amongst members of the same group is not a dangerous issue because all members of the same group obey the same equitable law. Divergence of interest of different countries is dangerous because there is no equitable law by which all countries abide.

Even were an equitable international law to be invented, there is no organization or entity to enforce it. And even if such a body were to come into existence, it could not possibly enforce this law on the most powerful nations because they are simply stronger than any enforceable body, especially if two or more major countries unite.

As long as the majority of the citizens of a country are law-abiding, law and order have a chance of being implemented. Law and order have no chance of being implemented at an international level, this is where "Might is Right" reigns supreme.

Each country is trying to be mighty in order to gain the possibility to act as they please. In the process, being mighty is an extremely expensive endeavor; it only leads to diverting resources away from human development and into human destruction. What a waste of valuable resources for all of us!

WHAT'S IN IT FOR THE STRONG?

As said before, the strong cannot guarantee their position in the future. This fact is not enough in itself to convince today's powerful nations to unite with the other weaker ones.

The strong nations of today feel invincible, or at least feel that they have worked hard enough to be where they are today, and have the right to reap the benefits of their hard work and ingenuity in all aspects. They want to keep being independent and successful.

I am aware that neither I nor other far greater writers could ever write would change the present mind of powerful nations and induce them to unite. What will change their mind is time.

Time does not only change people's minds on an issue, it also has the ability to change people's mindsets.

A person who perceives life as a daily struggle, as an arena where the strong take it all, is different from someone whose mindset revolves around the idea that life is a gift, that the best things in life are free, that you cannot be a loser because you are fortunate just to be alive, and in a way we have already won by being alive.

It is worth noting that the two mind sets are not mutually exclusive: one can oscillate between them at different phases of one's life. However, if we talk about the general trend in history, I tend to believe that humankind is approaching the second mindset and departing from the first. I have no proof for such a belief of course. My lack of such a proof is, as I said before, the fact that I do not believe in proving or disproving anything.

The second mindset—where the human being feels so rich with what he or she already has, and that it will be great to have extra things—will discourage greed and make people far more relaxed with their lives than they are today, especially in the technologically advanced countries.

So, the question is not "what's in it for the strong?" The strong needs to ask himself: "what's in it for us?" This question will come up when the mindset of the human being as a whole changes with time. The weak will also have to ask: "what's in it for us?" Unless both ask themselves this question, uniting the world is a hopeless case.

WHAT'S IN IT FOR US?

Let's use the metaphor of nature as the infrastructure of all living things. It is obvious that when the quality of the global environment deteriorates, all living creatures suffer. In the same sense, a global government is the infrastructure of the society of all human beings, and as long as this global government does not exist, all human beings will suffer.

What can a global government do that a system of multiple nations cannot?

If the world reaches a system of one global government, then all human beings will have a much better sense of security than they have today. Today's sense of security in each country has two sources: an internal and an external one.

The internal source stems from the feeling of the citizens that they belong to one country, have a bond with their fellow citizens, and that serving their own country will in effect serve themselves.

The external sense of security is based on each country's feeling that it can defend itself against external aggression using whatever diplomatic or military resources it has. This sense of security depends on the military power of each country. It varies widely, and some countries' internal sense of security is sometimes affected by external interference or aggression from other countries.

The sense of external security or insecurity in a world under one global government is eliminated because there are no countries to threaten the internal security. The only threat to internal security comes from inside the system itself.

The technological advances of today are at an acceptable level for a global government—should it ever exist—to make sure that the law is upheld on a global basis.

Today's human being is not ready to live in a global nation because of its state of mind. This is what needs to be worked on.

In a way, we can say that a global government gives all human beings an equal feeling of security. It makes me wonder whether human rights organizations share my view that the inherent right of all human beings to feel secure is violated by the mere fact that we live in a world of multiple nations.

Back to trying to shed some light on what a global government can do that a system of multiple nations cannot: After we have talked briefly about the sense of global security, the second issue that I would like to bring up is the ability of a global government to manage the environment on a global basis.

It is difficult for me to be convinced that the overall result of today's management of the global environment in our system of multiple nations is a satisfactory one.

Under the ruling of one global government the accountability of the effect of the human being on the global environment lies with one body—the global government—then, as with other issues, the level of civilization of the human race as a whole will determine the progress made on this issue. As things are going today, all countries blame others for such destruction while using each other's products, knowing that manufacturing or using these products in a not so environmentally friendly way inflicts damage on the environment. What a hypocritical position all countries are taking. The sad thing is that all can get away with it.

This will lead us to a more conceptual general statement of what a global government can do that a system of multiple nations cannot.

A global government has a better global decision making process on an issue or set of issues, and has a better ability to apply a decision on a global basis. It democratizes the life of the human being, without taking away his rights.

Taking the first part of the previous paragraph, one can safely assert that today's brains are used inefficiently, to say the least. There are many human beings on earth today that have superior intelligence, and others have great wisdom or a great sense of justice and compassion, and they are not contributing at all to the development of humanity as a whole. In the best cases, their effect is confined to certain groups or countries. However, while it is good for such countries to be fortunate in using their talents, these brains should have the chance to contribute to the whole of humanity in order for humankind to benefit and advance on the beautiful journey of existence and consciousness.

Again the reason for such inefficiency lies in our system of multiple nations.

While some countries are capable of benefiting from the talents of their citizens in the best way possible, many countries are not.

When people live under one global government where education, medical care, and equal opportunities are provided, the chances of the development of humankind will vastly increase, and the stage will be set for what I have labeled the third phase of development of humankind.

The decision making process on any issue is better once we live in a global government not only because superior brains are efficiently utilized, but also because the jurisdiction and scope of thinking is the globe. This does not mean that decisions become centralized, nor that democracy is being compromised; on the contrary, democracy is globalized.

Not only is the decision being 'globalized,' but so is the execution. A global government can better execute decisions that have a global effect, such as decisions concerning the environment, or global security, or the world economy. After the decision is made and is executed, it can better decide whether the decision was the right one, it can also better revise the decision based on the results and observations obtained on a global basis.

In today's political environment, the implementation of a decision reached by multiple nations is not ideal. Some countries are better than others in all the phases of making, implementing, monitoring, or revising a decision. Due to the variance between the abilities of different nations, the overall effect of any decision that is global in nature is being diluted, whether this decision has to do with the global economy, the global environment, or global security.

The execution of decisions made collectively by nations will almost always leave some not committing themselves to such a decision. This will create many loopholes for all kinds of abuse.

There are still points to discuss about what is in it for *us* if we unite. One of them is to ask ourselves what kind of a global government we are talking about. Another important point is to define how to make people think in a frame of mind implying *us* rather than *me*. The last point deals with the problem from the individual and country perspective.

LET US IMAGINE

We have repeatedly mentioned the expression "world government" without giving it much explanation until now. It is wise to give some general idea of what is meant by "world government." At the same time, we should be careful not to be too specific in our description to the point where we end up with one perspective of a world government that might not necessarily be the right version that is suitable for the future.

Once I have given a description of the general mental frame of the human being living under a "world government," I would like to touch on the general structure of this world government.

The foundation of today's democracy is to have multiple centers of power. This basic requirement is necessary for the evolution of our global society. History has proved on many occasions that whenever all power originates from one source in a specific society this spells trouble for such a society.

In a global government, one would think of power divided into a legislative, a judicial, and an executive branch, all performing checks and balances with each other.

The jurisdiction of the world government is the whole world. However, not all issues are discussed and decided upon at the level of the world government, and the world government has the right to override any law it deems contradictory to its duties.

The duties of the world government are as follows:

- To create a global set of laws.
- To uphold the law on a global basis.
- To protect the global environment.
- To provide an equal opportunity environment for all citizens.
- To establish an economic system where minimum requirements of a decent living standard are provided for all citizens.
- To provide global security for all citizens.

Now it is beneficial to touch upon each duty of the global government that we are imagining.

A Global set of laws is a must for the basic equality of all human beings on this earth. All human beings need to be treated equally under the law.

Upholding the law on a global basis means that there are issues that are the jurisdiction of the global government, issues such as diseases like cancer or AIDS, that are not region specific, or security issues that are related to groups that are involved in mass destruction activities, etc.

Protecting the global environment is an important duty; the global government has the right to regulate any activity that it finds harmful to the global environment.

Providing an equal opportunity environment for all citizens is a prerequisite for justice. No law is allowed that differentiates between people based on their place of origin, the color of their skin, their political views, or their income level.

By raising taxes, the global government redistributes wealth between the rich and the poor. All citizens of the world have to have access to globally uniform and good education, medical care, and other benefits that the global government sees proper to give its citizens.

The world has only one currency and a global central bank. One of the jobs of the global central bank is to decide on the interest rate of such a currency, depending on the global economy.

People can move anywhere and work anywhere on the globe, there is no need for a passport, because there are no ports to be passed.

The global government has the responsibility of providing global security, which is a necessary but not sufficient condition for the human being to develop.

Today no one holds the global security of the world. Strong as well as weak countries are wide open to threats from other countries or from groups that may in the future obtain weapons of mass destruction. It is not realistic to assume that such weapons will not be used or produced by groups or countries that will have the possibility to do so.

Let us not forget that weapons of mass destruction have been used in the past. Our system of multiple nations provides a good platform for conflicts to brew and burst in an uncontrollable fashion.

Today's economically and militarily strong cannot feel safe because they lack the ability to control to a satisfactory level the activities of other countries or groups that are producing, obtaining or utilizing weapons of mass destruction.

A global government has the ability and jurisdiction to do just that. Nothing is one hundred percent guaranteed, but the possibility to eliminate such a threat will be higher than it is today.

Perhaps security will be one of the important dividends that today's strong countries would reap from changing our system.

The world will be divided into geographical regions administered by a local administration, and this administration could have a political structure that mirrors that of the global government. The jurisdiction of the local administrations and their duties are set by the global government.

Half the key officials of the local administrations are

elected by the people of each region, and the other half are appointed by the global government.

The main theme is coherence, synergy, and non-contradictory responsibilities between all official bodies.

GLOBAL SECURITY

Back in 1990 or '91, I was watching CNN in the United States; the program was some kind of a meeting of experts from a few American security agencies. They had a map of the world in front of them and there were circles all over it.

These circles represented the ranges of some kinds of missiles that other countries or groups have, and they were saying that the range of these missiles had been increasing with time.

I remember I felt a little insecure at the time, and a thought came to my mind that it is possible to deter a rational enemy, because a rational enemy will know if he inflicts damage on others, others will inflict damage on him in return. However, my insecurity stemmed from my doubt about deterring an irrational enemy that is capable of inflicting damage on others without fear of retaliation. At the same time there is a possibility that a rational enemy in some instances would act irrationally.

I cannot, by any measure, be labeled as a security expert since my knowledge of weapons of mass destruction amounts to what I watch on TV, but I believe that one does not need to be an expert or even possess above average intelligence to conclude from the program I was watching that the range of the missiles they were talking about would continue to increase.

The failure of the security agencies to prevent such missiles from falling into the possession of the wrong hands allows us to extrapolate this situation in the future, and conclude that they will fail in the future as they have failed in the past.

Here I should mention that by failure I mean the success rate of prevention is less than one hundred percent, because whether a human being is killed by a hundred weapons from a hundred different sources or by one weapon from one source is irrelevant.

Furthermore, it is safe to assume that the strength, variety, effectiveness, availability, and ability of usage of conventional and mass destruction weapons will increase in the future. This increase will accompany the increase of the ability of non-rational groups or countries to obtain and use such weapons.

It is my belief that the effectiveness of all the good efforts done today and in the future to prevent conventional and mass destruction weapons from being used will be in vain due to the fact that our system of multiple nations prevents such effectiveness from being realized.

Indeed, the security of both the human being and the environment on a global basis will be the hostage of the weak and the strong. In other words, the number of players, rational or irrational, who can threaten the global security of the human being and the environment, is increasing. Our political system encourages the number of potential threats to increase because by default it puts human beings in different competing camps.

They compete to gain more power. They have no choice because unless we are all "us," each group needs power to prevent potential threats from other groups and each group constantly needs more and more power.

The human race has reasonably succeeded in regulating the quest for power on the group level. The challenge is to extrapolate such a success to a global level.

No amount of law enforcement agencies is enough to enforce the law in a country where citizens do not wish to abide by the law. The law in any country is abided by primarily because citizens wish to do so; it is a voluntary act. Law enforcement efforts come as a secondary reason, and are concentrated on the minority elements of a society that do not wish to abide by the law.

In a few countries the quest for power is being self-regulated by citizens that do not consider themselves successful in obtaining power unless it is done by lawful means. On an international level, international law is abided by only in the case were powerful nations agree to do so, or agree to enforce it on others, and the UN is only effective if it has the backup of powerful nations.

Powerful nations as well as weak ones always follow their national interest; many times this national interest as perceived by each nation is not in accordance with the interest of the human species or the global environment as a whole.

This situation is labeled in political science as a state of anarchy. The only way out is through unity.

Global security is an illusion for all countries, unless the world is under one global government.

The main reason for the possibility of achieving success in providing security for mankind under a global government is the feeling that is generated inside the human being when he or she believes in being part of one family.

The mother is only a mother with her own son, and a son is only a son with his own mother.

The feeling of belonging is not only a necessary condition for security, it is also a way of life.

We all live in families, and only the unfortunate ones do not. No matter what the outcome of the future might be, whether the model of the family is to continue to exist, or is abolished altogether, the basic need to feel safe and feel that one belongs has to be satisfied.

This need to feel safe is not satisfied in many parts of the world, and even where it is, due to our system of multiple nations, it can always be violated due to external threats that cannot be stopped in the long run.

Only in a system of global government do people feel they are being given an equal chance in life. This does not entirely eliminate non-rational threats from certain groups; however, it will bring these groups to a minimum, and at the same time the global jurisdiction of security forces will make it easier to eliminate them.

While on vacation in Bulgaria in 1999, I met a Russian journalist. I was discussing with her the situation in Russia and mentioned that in my opinion the solution for Russia's problems in the long run was to join the European Union. I was not surprised when she replied that Russia does not need such integration because Russia is a very rich country.

I realized what I already knew: Convincing countries to unite, without taking the particularities of each into account, is a very difficult task. I only hope that the union of the world comes about in a non-violent way, and part of the reason for writing this essay is to avoid just that.

EQUAL GLOBAL OPPORTUNITY

This is a tough nut to crack. I have known countries where the laws are non-discriminating while the actions of the major part of its citizens are, at least on a few issues, such as discrimination based on national/ethnic origin.

Equal global opportunity does not mean just having non-discriminating laws; global citizens need to have access to a uniform high quality educational system, as well as a high quality health care system. Education needs to be compulsory to a certain age.

TOO MANY

No vision has a slight chance of being realized unless it addresses population increase in the world.

The world has too many people. This needs to be controlled. Here the benefit of a global government is really felt. Since the jurisdiction of such a government is on a global basis, education is directed globally towards controlling population growth.

The main point is that global jurisdiction makes it possible for population control policies to succeed.

Managing population growth and the environment on a global basis are extremely important objectives; the main thrust of the solution is to provide the best education possible for all the world population. Clearly, management of the environment and population growth is a failure today on a national and international level.

If a bird has a good idea I want to hear it.

ON THE ROAD

Let us try to formulate a strategy about how to realize our vision. Now we are talking about how to move from where we are to where we want to be. We have many possibilities.

We might just say that the world is moving on the right path at the right speed and all we have to do is to wait.

I tend to believe the world will reach a stage where all countries will unite, but I do not believe this unification will be done in a smooth way. I have a feeling it will be done in an unjust way: The predators of the world might opt for unification because it facilitates domination.

Somehow, if there are no proper guidelines for unification, the outcome might be that, in that unified world, the majority of human beings will be dominated by a handful of others.

This outcome may be even worse than our political system today because it will permanently divide the world into "the haves" and "the have nots."

I would like to talk a little bit about the internet.

When graduate students used to develop their internet

applications, the idea of giving free access to information was very much a common theme and even once the internet got commercialized the culture of giving lots of things for free continued.

What is important to note is that the early developers of the internet in universities affected the path of the internet even when it got commercialized.

Other developers might have envisioned an internet with much less free information.

In the same way, we see that the early developers of Communism affected its path just because they were the creators. Other creators might have envisioned a Communist system with a less centralized economy.

In the same sense, we are trying to develop a vision of a unified world such that, if it happens one day, the outcome of our vision will have a positive effect, and be to the benefit of all human beings.

In this sense, leaving the future to unfold itself without interference in shaping the vision of a unified world is not an acceptable option for me. Creating a vision with major, clear features, but with enough room for maneuverability, is a wise thing to do.

Let us look again at the European Union and find out if we can learn something from such an experience.

So far the independence of each country is being maintained: Political decisions still lie with each country, and only when all countries in the EU decide to transfer part of their power to a common body, such as the European Parliament, is the power shift done.

On the other hand there is a common currency called the Euro. The effect of creating a common currency that has replaced many European currencies, especially the German Mark and the French Franc, is far-reaching.

What we can benefit from the European Union experience in order to qualify for world union is as follows.

The fact that Europe is uniting gives a push to our vision, because countries are already doing what we are calling for.

The unification of different countries in Europe is not being done by countries that have been on good terms throughout history—quite the contrary. That European experience might encourage us to foresee unification between countries that are fighting today.

The military, economic, technological, demographic and other characteristics of the countries in the EU are different, yet there is no feeling among members that the strong are dominating the weak. In fact, part of the reason to unite is to integrate the strong in the Union so that they do not try to dominate the weak ones if they are kept separate.

Equally important strong countries are convinced to unite

with weaker ones; in fact the strong countries in the Union have been spearheading it, namely France and Germany.

The last two paragraphs are very important for our vision because, as said before, each member country benefits more from belonging to the Union than from being separate, regardless of the power level of each country.

One can argue that Europe's experience cannot be generalized to encompass all the countries of the globe. The answer for such an argument is that the common factor between all countries is that every citizen is a human being. I believe, in the long run, that this simple but basic fact will be the main drive for global unification.

I am glad logic is not the only faculty of the human brain—compassion is too.

If life is a car, then logic should be the chauffeur, and compassion the passenger.

It is true that the chauffeur decides on many aspects of the trip; however the passenger decides the destination.

THE GREATEST OBSTACLE

Let us think about the greatest obstacle that is in the way of unification.

There is no doubt in my mind that the greatest obstacle for global unification is the set of ideas in the brains of human beings today.

How can you convince a person who identifies himself as an Englishman, an American, or a Chinese, that it is far more important to identify oneself as a human being?

NATIONAL AND CULTURAL TOLERANCE

Each culture has a certain degree of tolerance towards foreign ideas and foreign behavior from within and from outside the culture.

It would be possible to compare such tolerance between different cultures, at least on a qualitative basis, but I leave it up to scholars to set such measures. However, the important point is that while people having a certain culture may happen to be extremely tolerant, we could find the policy of their nation may adopt extremely intolerant positions, for internal or external sets of reasons.

Often, in international politics, cultural and political tolerance are confused. Hostilities between two or more countries make the citizens of such countries act in an inhuman way towards each other; the same mother that cares for her baby in one country and loves children to death, wishes bombs to be dropped on another country as a way to eliminate the enemy, who is in her mind putting her and other babies of her country in danger.

If ever asked whether she approves of dropping bombs on the enemy that have a good chance of also killing babies, she might very well express disapproval. However, if the same mother is asked whether she approves of dropping bombs on the enemy, her answer might very well be positive.

The point that I am trying to make is that not only does nationalism push people to potentially become violent and act inhumanely towards other human beings that belong to other countries; it also puts citizens in an extremely confused state of mind.

Belonging to different nations automatically decreases the level of tolerance of all human beings due to the threats that are perceived to be coming from other countries.

As a matter of fact, in our system of multiple nations we are all enemies until the opposite is proven. At the same time we are all friends until the opposite is proven. And all the time we are all confused. Cultural tolerance or intolerance has been overridden by national considerations. While the cultural aspects of a nation might affect its international policies, usually nationalistic considerations based on perceptions regarding the nature of international policies are the dominant factors that shape the actions of a nation.

HOW TO GO FROM A TO B?

It might be a good idea to start by creating an international organization that clearly states that its purpose is to unify the world.

The initial efforts of such an organization will be to open branches in each country and explain to the officials of each country its peaceful mission. It will be necessary to start by stating that the purpose of that organization won't be to challenge or interfere with the internal politics of any country, nor will it be to work outside the acceptable political system of any country. That organization will plant the idea of a global nation, and invite everyone to contribute to it.

It will also invite the intellectuals who oppose the idea to contribute to the discussion and highlight the weaknesses of such a vision, and the strengths or rightness of their own visions.

At the same time this organization, as any, will need to enlist as many members as possible and raise funds in order to conduct a marketing plan for its views in each country.

Although all the organization's branches need to have the maximum possible ability to operate in each country, the idea of a global nation and of reaching such a target in a non-violent way will need to be abided by by all branches or members.

If any member does not abide by these two principles then he or she will be asked to leave the organization. It is only natural to expect different members to have different views and develop different strategies to reach the ultimate objective; however, these differences should only be tolerated on condition that the ultimate objective will be reached in a non-violent way.

It is important to develop strategies for such an organization. An initial strategy would be to concentrate on the intellectuals and powerful people in each country, another would be to concentrate on the masses, and a third strategy would be to split efforts in both directions.

Depending on the conditions and political structure of each country such strategies could well be developed by each branch. What is important is that the unification process is to be done by the governments themselves and not by the organization. The organization will help to focus and facilitate the efforts and provide intellectual help for the unification process, thus patience is required.

It would be stupid for a teacher to hurt his student if he does not learn the lesson.

After this organization has reached a certain development stage, publications and strategies will start flowing from its branches and members, and since the structure of this organization will be a loose one, it will have no problem if other members join other organizations, as long as other organizations are peaceful in nature and have the common good as their objective.

If a person belongs to an organization that preaches nationalism and rejects unification, then he can attend certain meetings of the organization, and he will be given the status of a friend of that organization. Obviously this person would not be allowed to vote in the organization.

It needs to be clear that this organization does not seek power, nor does it seek for any one of its members to be in power, although members are free to do so as far as permitted under each country's law. It seeks to stimulate discussion concerning a global nation and market the idea on a global basis; it also seeks to focus brainpower on a global basis to find the best way to achieve such a goal.

It is also important to precisely state that such an organization does not promote the union of countries in any specific region of the world. Any unification of countries needs to be seen in the context of global unification, and not as an end in itself.

Following are a few of the topics that will need to be discussed by such an organization:

1. The necessary conditions to make unification between two or more countries successful and irreversible.

2. To explain the phrase 'successful unification' and link it to concepts of justice and fairness.

3. To define the parameters that need to be considered in the unification of different countries or regions.

4. To apply those parameters to different countries and regions, and explore different scenarios.

5. To explore what might go wrong in the unification process, and assess how to avoid this process ending up as one of domination of the strong over the weak.

6. To create centers of study dedicated to producing publications endorsed by the organization, and to financially and intellectually help members who wish to produce such studies.

7. To create working teams in the organization. These teams would be involved in raising money, soliciting members, producing literature, marketing the concept, etc.

8. To develop the internal rules of the organization regarding the election process, organizational structure, responsibilities and authorities of key positions.

AM I NAÏVE?

You bet I am! All dreamers are, or else how could one change anything? Change is always a step in the unforeseen, yet not changing is also a step in the unforeseen, for by not changing one assumes that future conditions do not merit change. This is also a dream; we are all naïve, which is a good thing in my view.

WHO GETS WHAT?

Everyone needs to have free education, and free medical attention whenever needed. Some would argue that such social benefits are too costly and would eventually lead to the bankruptcy of any state that would provide adequate social benefits to its citizens.

The answer to such an objection is simple: Given the inefficiencies that will be eliminated by changing from a system of multiple nations to a system of a global nation, the sums of money that will be saved will be enough to cover such investments. Notice that I have labeled free medical care and free education as investments and not expenses; the reason is that making the most valuable asset in a society, the human being, better in mind and body is simply an investment with near- and far-future dividends.

The pressing question still remains: "How do we do that?"

One cannot deny that today's human beings live in countries that have extremely different standards of living. The objective of globalization is not to redistribute the wealth of countries, but rather to enhance the wealth of all the human species, and better the conditions of life on earth.

Thus, how to go from A to B is not clear. It needs the will of many, not only mine. Let's hope this essay helps in gathering this will, and paves the way.

NATION STATE INEFFICIENCIES

We have talked about the inefficiencies that will be eliminated by switching from multiple states to a global state. Let us list a few of these inefficiencies.

The most obvious one is the expenditure of each nation on its army. The amount of money spent to buy weapons liabilities rather than assets and maintain armies, as well as engage in international wars from time to time, is unbelievable.

If we suppose that the human species had succeeded in abolishing the system of multiple nations before World Wars I and II, we can imagine the amount of suffering and destruction that could have been avoided and the waste of resources in money as well as in human capital that could have been spared.

The argument that war motivates great inventions is not acceptable because in times of peace far greater inventions have been achieved as a whole.

The second inefficiency is the waste of human capital.

It is absolutely essential for the success of the human race to give a chance to all its members to contribute to their development. One cannot know where the next genius that will push the envelope of knowledge will be born. It is safe to assume that many geniuses may have been denied their essential contribution to the human species because they lived in countries that consume rather that produce technologies.

Technologically advanced countries know that behind every leap in technology or basic science, there are smart people at work. Even when it is teamwork this does not deny the contribution of superb brains in each team; many times such brains are those of immigrants from technologically deprived countries. One can only imagine that behind each immigrant who contributed to the development of science and technology in foreign countries there are many geniuses that stayed in their technologically deprived countries and did not have the chance to contribute to the human species.

Thus, in Darwin's language, by not giving part of its outstanding members the opportunity to contribute the human species is denying itself the possibility to maximize its chances of survival at the optimal level under the system of multiple countries.

The third inefficiency lies in the fact that we have been working on the wrong issues.

One can easily imagine, within any period of history, how people had to divert their resources from developing themselves to engaging in conflicts with other nations—whether it was a full blown conflict or a more subtle one that diverted lots of resources for a long period of time.

THE UNIVERSAL COCKROACH

The fourth is the inefficiency of having a limited jurisdiction and a narrow vision.

Countries are unable to properly address interrelated issues such as security, the environment, education, health, technological advancements, living standards, global population growth, and so on, simply because there is a wrong assumption that such issues can be dealt with on a national or international level.

Advanced countries assume that their technological advancement, their economic prowess and their democratic systems enable them to enjoy a high level of security. This assumption is unfounded, simply because if the gap in any society, whether advanced or not, between the "haves" and the "have-nots" is big, and if the acceptable standard of living is only enjoyed by a few, then this is a recipe for social upheaval. Once this reality becomes common knowledge it can readily be deduced that it is not possible to sustain a system of multiple nations where a few nations enjoy a good standard and many do not.

The above statement does not mean that it is the job of technologically advanced countries to take care of non-technologically advanced ones. In fact, countries that have been successful in contributing positively to the advancement of the human being need to be cherished. The idea is not to kill the goose that lays golden eggs by overburdening it with responsibilities that are beyond its capabilities, but to increase the number of geese that lay golden eggs. However, we need to put them in one farm.

In today's economy a few countries are consuming energy at an alarming rate. While greed works if your sole objective is to make money, greed does not work if the human species has multiple objectives.

It is a major obsession for deprived countries to think that their ultimate objective is to live the life of technologically advanced countries; they have somehow lost the compass that each society had developed of what is wrong and what is right. It seems today that "greed is good, greed is beautiful" is the new compass—but luckily not for everyone.

It seems to me that unless the human species is under a system of global government, it will not be able to solve its problems, it will not be able to sustain its oases of democracy and technological advancements.

THE TROJAN HORSE

The question still rests on how to prevent the creation of a powerful few from abusing our system of global government in order to control the whole human species in such a way that we end up with a global system where the few enjoy all the goodies and the many are simply deprived and at their mercy.

I have to admit that this is one of the major weaknesses of a capitalist system: Unless we are absolutely sure that resources are channeled into free education and healthcare, we might end up with a system where the powerful few dominate and abuse the many, thus the idea of a global government becomes the Trojan Horse that will be used by the fittest to dominate.

It is not surprising that after Russia stopped pursuing Communism we started hearing about exploring different versions of Capitalism.

In today's world there is a Capitalist and technologically advanced country that has an embarrassing number of its people homeless, and there is another with a sophisticated social system for its citizens.

The concept that free education and healthcare need to be provided for all human beings and is a necessity for the welfare of the human species as a whole is not an easy concept to sell.

I was surprised to find out that in some technologically advanced countries such an issue is not settled; in fact, it is one of the major dividing lines between different parties.

There are two lines of thought: One says it is important to provide free education and healthcare and that this can be thought of as an investment in the human being that will widely pay off in the future in terms of quality of the citizen that will reflect on all aspects of the nation's life. The other line of thought considers providing such a service for the citizen as an expenditure that is too heavy to bear and that the results are negative because it diverts resources from other much needed areas such as capital expenditure, where with time it is such capital expenditure that will make the economy expand, and provide jobs for people; thus people will be able to afford healthcare and good education.

I tend to believe that in a well thought out system of global government, all human beings could afford free education and healthcare, because the resources needed will come from reduction on expenditure on armies and their hardware globally, it will also come from the ability of a global government to better match its revenues and expenses, especially that the risk of an all out war between two countries will be eliminated.

This means a global government can afford to teach and provide medical care for its citizens, and at the same time there are enough resources left in private and public funds for capital expenditure and other necessary requirements to run an efficient government.

THE UNIVERSAL COCKROACH

It is difficult today for a nation, no matter how powerful or technologically advanced, and no matter how hard working its citizens are, to achieve a good level of human development for them. To start with, each nation has to take care of its armed forces in order to make sure it is reasonably safe from other countries' threats.

One only has to read the history of the twentieth century to realize how difficult a task this is for rich nations, let alone poor ones.

Not only do nations continue to divert resources to their armed forces, but military hardware also needs to be maintained and becomes obsolete with time. Thus it needs to be replaced.

The problem does not stop at the level of expenditure on military hardware and personnel. The nature of the external threat to each country is not always easy to be defined or agreed upon. Even with the break up of the Soviet Union, each nation—whether rich or poor—still finds it difficult to assess the nature of the future enemy, and thus the kind of weapons and military needed. This exerts a never-ending pressure to continuously invest in the armed forces of each country.

It is perfectly understandable how a technologically advanced country is unable to spend as much money as it really intends on education and healthcare and other social programs, or maybe to improve the infrastructure of the nation, feeling that such money is needed to ensure the security of the nation.

The problem does not end here: We have only talked about the amount of resources that need to be diverted. We need to point out that as in a successful business, income is not the only important factor to worry about, but cash flow management is equally, if not more, important.

If a nation is suddenly attacked by other nations, or an immediate claim is being put on its armed forces to be engaged in some military operation, then resources are suddenly diverted and previous social programs are suddenly stopped in order to ensure the necessary cash needed for the military operations. Some nations start borrowing money that is burned in the battlefields, thus the economic prosperity suffers and human development in such countries comes to a halt and may even start on a reverse path.

The trade off between bread and arms is only one aspect of our system of multiple nations.

Let us divert our attention to envision what kind of common education we need to give our global citizens.

Can we specify the sets of beliefs that need to be shared by the human species and that are absolutely necessary for the success of our endeavor?

EDUCATION VERSUS SPECIALIZATION

While living in technologically advanced countries I was impressed by the level of specialization their citizens enjoy; it is entirely possible to find people who are authorities or experts on a certain subject or technology. This fact definitely leads to pushing the envelope of knowledge and technology further. I was not happy to find out that this level of specialization is not without a consequence.

It seems that the more citizens specialize in their role in society the more they become ignorant in other unrelated fields: They seem to develop a case of narrow vision.

There is an underlying assumption that in order for a society to be technologically advanced and economically prosperous it is enough for each citizen to be good in one profession. Beyond this requirement citizens are not really expected to know much about different subjects, unless it is their interest to do so.

This situation leads to citizens that are well informed in a few subjects and ignorant in many. The problem rises when it comes to election day and selecting the top people in a country.

The fact that people do not have enough knowledge on different subjects makes it very difficult to elect and control the political body that is running the country.

The agenda of politicians to win the election by necessity trickles down to generalities, and leads to political maneuvers that have nothing to do with real issues. The sad story is that in today's technologically advanced countries officials are elected based on everything except their political agendas, and this is directly related to the complexity of the issues involved and the lack of necessary knowledge among ordinary citizens in order to make an educated decision concerning who to vote for.

People trust the politicians to do a good job, and often the ignorance of the people in general makes it possible for lobbies and special groups to seize and shape the opinion of the masses in a way that most of the time these masses will depend on opinion leaders to tell them whether the politicians are doing a good job or not. Most of the time these opinion leaders have special interests and are moved or influenced by them. It is not surprising that all over the world the media is being controlled. One of the sources of democracy is multiple sources of independent information and analysis, but this goes out of the window. Ignorance of the masses is especially noticeable where knowledge of foreign policy is concerned, because national policy is more easily comprehended by the masses since they feel it is more related to their daily life.

In a world where the level of cultural interaction is exploding, one can hardly stress the importance of all citizens of the world to have adequate knowledge of world history and geography, as well as world cultures. It is not acceptable, as is the case today among citizens of each country, to stereotype other countries or cultures.

This stereotyping, which is based on ignorance, has far overreaching negative effects on everyone, making it essential to provide adequate information for citizens of different countries about one another.

Why would anyone be interested in knowing about others who are considered inferior?

This is again a problem that technologically advanced countries suffer from; this problem is common in the history of mankind: All powerful societies considered their civilization to be superior; force was the litmus test that proved such a perception to be true or false.

While this test is a natural one, and not far from what the law of the jungle dictates, the human being must once and for all draw the line between the origin of the human species and where this species is going. Modern concepts in evolutionary psychology might be helpful for us to understand the effect of our past evolutionary experiences on our thinking today; thus some preprogrammed reactions imbedded in our minds built from historic experiences might be falsely and dangerously triggered to face a modern problem.

It might very well be that we are still adopting a preemptive and aggressive stand towards each other that not only is unjustified, but moreover dangerous and harmful for our future as a human species.

If the philosophical answer to where we are going is forever dictated by our origin in the animal kingdom, then it is futile to imagine or try to create a more peaceful and fair world for everyone. Yet if this is the case, how come notions such as justice, fairness, compassion and so on have evolved through history?

I tend to romanticize about the possibility of an exit for us from being forever living in a world where might is right, although I am unable to prove or disprove whether might is right or right is might. All we can do is work towards what we believe in. Naturally I believe in the notion that right is might, only one has to agree what is right and what is not. It is confusing, I know, this is why we need to have compassion as the passenger, and logic as the driver; we also need to make sure compassion and logic work smoothly together.

There is a need for the convergence of civilizations in order for our system of a global nation to work.

The question is: How can civilizations converge, and is such a process already underway?

BASIC LESSONS

To start with, all civilizations have a major common element, namely the human being. Due to advancements in technology the external environment is gradually becoming the same for all human beings on earth. One would object and note that although the external environment is becoming the same, the background of people is not the same and thus the human species will never belong to the same culture.

Let us look back at history. It is no secret that the seeds of many ideas that are common to the Western human being today came from the Greek civilization.

While this is true, it is not enough to stop at this point. Aristotle's student Alexander the Great went to occupy the Orient; he came back and declared himself the King-God. He was infected with the Oriental civilization and this idea spread in Europe, which is the "heir" of the Greek civilization.

To make things a little more complicated, the origin of the five major religions in the world—Hinduism, Judaism, Buddhism, Christianity, and Islam—lie in Asia. These religions—combined or separate—are also the religions of Western civilization, as it is commonly understood today.

It is interesting to note that not only did the idea of separation of religion and state originate, or was at least practiced in ancient Greece to some degree, but the Orient also produced the same idea when Jesus Christ answered the people who were trying to frame him by telling them to give to Caesar what is Caesar's and give to God what is God's.

Europe's emperors used this declaration by Jesus to fight the power of the Church when the Pope tried to claim power over earthly matters. Emperors felt that earthly matters were their jurisdiction and not the Church's.

While Greeks and Romans are considered today as part of the Western heritage, it is only a political matter to separate the Greek and Oriental civilizations: They are the same evolving civilization.

In the same manner, it is a political matter today to speak about the Western and Eastern civilizations: They are also the same civilization evolving. All civilizations constitute part of the civilization of the human being.

Any idea or thought that is produced by any human being belongs to the human species, claiming the idea to belong to this civilization or that, or this country or that is only playing politics, it is an attempt to gain a competitive edge in the "survival of the fittest" game.

Today the dividing lines between civilizations are becoming more blurry; countries that belong to the same civilization do not necessarily share the same perspective towards a wide range of matters and each country chooses its friends or its enemies using complex criteria that have something to do with difference of civilizations, but not everything.

A person who attended a university has more in common with another person half across the globe who also attended a university than his neighbor who did not.

Common Education is the Key to Making the Human Being Belong to One Civilization.

It is my conviction that we are continuously converging as societies and as civilizations. It is sad to see war still being one of the outcomes and tools for this convergence to take place, yet we need to remember what happened with ancient Sparta and Athens: The one that conquers by the sword is not necessarily the one who prevails.

It is true that the powerful adopts foreign ideas for his civilization and with time claims them to be his own. It is also true that it is difficult to know which thought originated in which civilization, but it is not important to know the origin of an enlightened thought, as much as it is important that this thought be adopted and spread to all humanity.

To cut the story short, I wish to say that civilizations will converge to a common civilization. This has always been the case since civilizations started to have contact with each other. The challenge is to minimize the need for domination and war during this process.

While we hope that the convergence of civilizations happens with the least possible violence, we are unable to foresee if this indeed will happen.

Having said that, as with any future project or vision, one needs to ensure proper planning and commitment for it to become a reality.

Indeed, Europe today, in most of its parts, gives free education and medical care to its citizens. This is no minor diversion from the survival principles adhered to in nature. I believe such a course will ultimately carry the day for Europe.

I do not feel at ease leaving the last paragraph unexplored: One needs to mention that the ideas of Karl Marx were behind the change that happened to western Europe, and which made some countries adopt a social system that gives free education and medical care to its citizens.

One does not need to jump to the conclusion that a country that does not have a good social safety net such as the United States is totally in error. To start with, their accomplishments on many fronts by the United States are no laughing matter. However, I believe that in a global system the human species can have it both ways: enough resources to have an advanced social system and a social safety net for all the citizens of the world, and at the same time adequately invest in the global business and technological environments.

PROBLEMS IN HEAVEN

I wonder sometimes why the idea of global integration is not such a popular one.

I would imagine people and organizations concerned about the environment to be in favor of having the human species belong to one political entity on the condition that it is in favor of environmentally friendly policies.

This will surely make the task of preserving the environment a much easier one, since the task of formulation, implementation and monitoring of environmental policies would be much simpler than today where one has to deal with a lot of countries.

On the other hand, how can one make sure that the global entity is not driven by private interest groups, as is the case today with many countries? That makes it impossible to have an environmentally friendly policy, thus, instead of having a situation where the environment is adequately preserved one ends up with a situation where it is being globally compromised.

This is indeed crucial for our vision of the entire human species being under one global entity to succeed.

This question needs to be addressed not only because of global environmental concerns, but also because special interest groups will try to sway decisions in their favor in almost all aspects of the society.

Even among countries where democracy is considered to be a fact of life, none has found a proper solution for this matter. This will make us face a formidable problem. Are we imagining a world where the human beings are put in a situation, where it is impossible to make sure that proper decisions are taken on a global level?

We need to be modest at this point and acknowledge the fact that there is no political system that could be invented that would ensure proper decision-making.

In case of a political system where the power is concentrated in one body or person, it is obvious that while the ability of this person to check the decisions of all under him or her is formidable, there is no one to check the soundness of the decisions made by the supreme ruler.

In the case of a system where power is distributed over many centers, such as between the legislative, executive and judicial bodies, this system is still susceptible to interest groups. Besides, governance is possible only by coalition, and if coalition is not possible then a gridlock or a stalemate occurs and everything comes to a halt.

Thus the solution of making sure that the right decisions are being made is not only a function of the political system being adhered to, but more so a function of the quality of the citizens that the global system governs.

BALANCE OF POWER

There is a common opinion today that since the Soviet Union has collapsed then the only superpower is the United States.

One forgets that the principle of the balance of power will eventually reveal itself as one of the most enduring principles in political theory since the beginning of any social interaction within the human race.

This principle states that parties will collaborate to weaken the strongest among them.

The parties may be part of the same family, or political groups in the same country, or indeed countries.

The level of collaboration among the weaker parties against the strongest might be of an economic nature, or political, and of course, in many cases, of a military nature.

This principle has been in play throughout history, and one only has to read some to find out how great powers have risen and have surely fallen—unfortunately almost always with great bloodshed involved.

Granting the opinion that great powers failed because of over-expansion is a valid one, yet the principle of balance of power is behind the fact that great powers had to simultaneously fight on many fronts because other powers collaborated to weaken them, thus reaching a stage where the revenues generated from their empires would be much less than the expenses shed; as a result their economies collapsed, and in turn their abilities to expand or hold their ground collapsed as well.

The only solution for such a dilemma is to create a system where everyone believes that they truly belong to the same society, and this can only be achieved on a global level by creating the global nation.

It is an illusion to believe that things can continue as they are today in our system of multiple nations without great suffering for people in many countries, rich or poor.

To start with, rich countries assume that they are able to control their destinies and continue to improve the welfare of their citizens, while the gap between them and poorer countries is widening and the gap between the different social groups of each country is becoming bigger. If it were extremely difficult to live in a society where the gap between the different social groups is wide, why would rich countries assume that they are able to live in a world with huge gaps between different countries?

There is no way, even with the best security organizations in each country to protect its citizens, to be able to live in a peaceful world where there is a wide gap between the living standards of different countries. The availability of weapons of mass destruction has already passed a threshold whereby it is no more the monopoly of a few countries; they have become a commodity readily bought and sold in the international markets. It is a scary thought, but one that needs to be addressed properly.

Thus, global security is more easily maintained if citizens of the world belong to one nation, not only because of the ability of security forces to ward off any global threat because they have global jurisdiction, but because citizens of the world all have a stake in a better life and the majority want to preserve what they have. Thus, global security is preserved primarily not by security forces but by global citizens who have a stake in preserving the peace, which is not the case today.

If the security of a country is being compromised, it is hard to imagine that the economy would not be compromised as well. A student of economics knows that it is difficult for a country to attract investments if it is considered to have significant political risks, let alone if there is a perception that its judicial system is not functioning well.

It seems that powerful nations tend to identify the solutions to the security threats that they are facing in terms of military operations, which might be of the preemptive type in foreign lands. While these operations are indeed capable of nipping in the bud any possible formation of activities or groups that might pose a threat to international security, they do not have the ability to stop such groups or operations from forming again.

It is like cutting grass: The lawn mowers that cut the grass have no ability to stop the soil from producing grass. The only way is to plant trees that have edible fruits. This way people will tend these trees and their shade will prevent grass from growing. Whatever is left of the grass that is able to grow in spite of the shade will be more easily dealt with.

Let's take this analogy and apply it to the citizens of the world: It is not a secret that the best way to channel the energy of the citizens of any country into productive means is to have a robust economy in order for the majority of them to have a stake in the political and economic stability.

However, the very fact that our global system is comprised of multiple nations makes it impossible for the majority of countries to achieve economic and political stability.

Few countries were able to provide a kind of a safety net that provides minimum living conditions for their citizens and at the same time maximize the ability for them all to grow and prosper.

Only in very few countries that have special situations was it possible for this safety net to be provided and for the ability to maximize the chances for their citizens to be realized. Having said that, even such countries were not immune from what happened around them at certain periods in their history.

Today the technological gap between a minority of countries—namely the United States, Europe, Japan, and to a lesser degree Australia and the "New Asian Tigers"—and the rest of the world is extremely big.

THE UNIVERSAL COCKROACH

It is not possible to achieve an acceptable level of global security and standard of living for the majority of countries under our system of multiple nations.

Countries that have a poor standard of living will threaten the security of others, and countries with a high technological base pose a formidable competitive barrier for others to cross in order to prosper.

IS IT TOO LATE?

In my opinion, due to the huge technological gap, and due to reasons related to the culture and demographics of different technologically poor countries, it is too late to expect developing countries to have a better standard of living in our system of multiple nations.

Indeed, in the long run the standard of living for citizens of countries such as India, China, and Middle and Far Eastern countries, as well as countries in South America, and others, will decline, all due to different reasons, but the most common reason being that the ability of such countries to produce technology—whether in the present or the future—cannot generate enough revenues to sustain their population increase in the future.

Notice here that we did not take the natural resources of each country into consideration. This is due to the fact that they are mostly perishable commodities and that the countries with the technology to extract them take a sizable share of the revenues generated from them; thus revenues from natural resources are shared with other countries and their beneficial effect on the owner country is minimized and diminishes with time.

If all the citizens of the world are under one political economical system, then no matter where the natural resources are or who extracts them—whether the private or the public sector or a combination of both—the revenues generated are taxed, and this tax goes to educate, hospitalize and shelter the citizens of the world.

In fact, not only are the revenues of the natural resources taxed, but also the revenues of every corporation and citizen of the world.

So, while the revenues produced today from technologically advanced countries have their profits taxed and their benefits go to the citizens of these countries, at the same time, part of the revenues produced from extracting the natural resources in countries that import technology go to the technologically advanced countries. Add to that the fact that the money that belongs to wealthy citizens and even governments of developing countries is in the banks of technologically advanced countries instead of being invested in these developing countries due to the lack of a proper investment environment, and you can see how the gap gets wider.

Today the implicit position that technologically advanced countries hold is that, because of the hard work of the citizens of such countries, success has been achieved, and it is only fair that it be enjoyed by those who made it happen while the fortunes of other countries are mostly left to each country to chase.

Add to it the fact that, indeed, technological countries try to help less fortunate ones and, irrespective of the reasons of such assistance it is still to be appreciated. Only such a position taken by technologically advanced countries has certain consequences that we will spell out. But before doing so, let's talk about the position taken by developing countries.

The countries that are not technologically advanced are trying to leverage themselves by using the technology needed to build their infrastructures, such as transportation systems, power generating plants, etc. from other countries.

The ability of these countries to understand the imported technology is limited; the imported technology is consumed like food, and the need to continuously import new technologies is never ending, while their ability to produce home grown technologies is at best limited.

The problems do not stop here, because even if developing countries succeed in providing proper infrastructure for their citizens, a question remains; what could these countries produce and sell? The answer is not much; this is due to the fact that their societies are unable to produce technologies at a pace that would sustain an acceptable standard of living.

The fact of the matter is that a factory is a place to produce a value added product, and it is a non-perishable source of income, as well as sustaining the lives of its employees. But for all that to happen factories need to apply technologies that produce internationally competitive products, especially since world trade agreements are opening more and more of the boundaries of all countries for foreign competition; thus the possession of competitive technology is crucial for the success of any country, and developing countries are unable to produce such technologies.

It seems logical at this stage to conclude that the solution is for countries to obtain technologies in order to build factories (that produce goods or services) that are internationally competitive.

It's just that the solution is impossible to achieve. The reason is that the technological gap is very big and the competition is fierce—the capitalist system of our system of multiple nations produces what we have today: very rich countries and very poor countries, and the cliché is very true: the poor get poorer and the rich get richer, not only between countries; but also within countries.

One might argue that it is not the duty of successful countries that worked very hard in developing their social, economic and political systems to help other countries that many times seem corrupt and lazy to have a better standard of living.

If one looks at it from a moral point of view, it is not convincing to ask successful countries to help others, mainly because the moral obligations for successful countries are towards their citizens in the first place. However, one has to build an argument that it is to the advantage of technologically successful countries to work for abandoning our system of multiple nations. In fact, we need to build convincing arguments for all countries to do so, and not only rich ones.

THE CONSEQUENCE OF THE STATUS QUO

Let us say we continue living in our world of multiple nations; as things are going right now, countries that have the largest population in number are under intense pressure to sustain or halt the deterioration in the standard of living of their citizens. Countries such as China, India or Egypt will suffer from a continuous deterioration of the standard of living of their citizens. The theory of a sustainable middle class forming in such countries is an illusion; ultimately these societies will have very powerful rich minorities and a very weak poor majority.

This fact is not a reflection of the inability of their politicians to find adequate solutions to their demographic problem, rather it is a reflection of the fact that in our system of multiple nations it is somewhat impossible for countries with huge populations to sustain their standard of living—it is economically and politically impossible to solve internal problems and at the same time address security issues that have to do with external threats.

In other words, the human species needs every improvement possible, and any possible complication removed in order to barely make it.

The majority of the most highly populated countries will

become poor with rich minorities, and the rest will be rich with an acceptable middle class.

The end result being rich countries living in fortresses and exchanging goods and services between each other, and poor countries living in misery and plotting day and night how to hurt the rich countries because they think they are the reason for their misery even if they are not.

In such a scenario, because the environment is a hostage in every country, rich or poor, poor countries will find the environment a bargaining chip in their hands (you may call it blackmail) in order to have some money from the rich countries in exchange for preserving their local environment in such a way as not to harm the global environment.

Once in a while groups will use weapons of mass destruction in a violent way to hurt rich and poor countries, and rich countries will find themselves forced to conduct military operations in foreign lands in order to thwart the actual and potential security breaches of their fortresses.

In short, life becomes terrible with a lot of violence involved, and ultimately the sophisticated economies of the technologically advanced countries cannot sustain major security breaches for a long time: Their standard of living will start to deteriorate and this will lead to the misery of the human race.

TRANSITORY PERIOD

Let us imagine how the transition between where we are now and where we want to be could take place.

The European Union is expanding throughout Eastern Europe; ultimately Russia will join the European Union. Once this happens, China, the Far East, and the Middle East will become the next possible regions for integration. At this point, the US and western hemisphere will not be ready to join, simply because the United States feels it has no need to join such a union and it perceives it as an economical threat more than an ideological possibility to unite the world.

At this stage the European Union, which still embodies mainly European countries that are perceived to have a common culture or at least a common background, will start to engage in a soul searching discussion of whether to see itself as a European entity or as a global entity with a European nucleus or origin. Perhaps this process has already started with the possible unification of Turkey, that is both an Eastern and Western country.

At this stage China and India will be suffering from a case of over population, and will have depleted all their options in raising the standard of living of their populations. At the same time, certain advancements in biotechnology and communications technology will further assist the integration process.

If today people are unable to choose what their children will look like, in the future it may become a possibility. Once this happens a Chinese, an Indian or a Swedish citizen will have the option to choose how his or her daughter will look, thus the way people look like will not be traced to a certain region in the world any more. Coupled with the explosion in communication this will ultimately help to build a common universal culture.

These two advancements, in tandem with a pressing need to solve the economic and demographic problems of China and India, together with an emerging new ideology to unite the world, would make it possible for the European Union to expand eastward; at this stage three countries will be watching the scenario that is unfolding.

These three countries are Great Britain, the United States and Japan.

Great Britain will most probably be the first one to join this union whole-heartedly. The reason for waiting so long is that as usual its conservative attitude and special relationship with the United States, coupled with the fact of its geographic location as part of the European Union, will direct her to position herself at the crossroads so that if all goes well she will join, but if things go wrong she can maintain a safe distance. This historic position is going to change once India joins the European Union because India is the jewel in the crown for the once great British Empire, and the very thought of India as part of a union that encompasses all the European countries, as well as Russia, will tip the balance for Great Britain to fully join the Union.

Great Britain will be the country that will ultimately play an important role in convincing the United States to join such a union and Canada and South America will join sooner or later, leaving us with Japan.

As is well known in the business world, Japan considers its racial purity to be a source of power, and it considers America's racial diversity to be a source of weakness. As long as economic prowess is maintained Japan can afford to continue to think along these lines. However, confronting such a huge economic competitor that encompasses almost the whole world, will make Japan decide to join such a Union not based on ideological reasons, but rather on economic necessity.

During their modern history, the Japanese have contributed wonderfully to the advancement of the human civilization in the technological and business arena, together with China. Once the Global Union is achieved the Japanese and Chinese cultural heritage will be of most help to the world civilization.

As far as the Middle East is concerned I can imagine countries would join the Global Union country by country. I would imagine the first ones to do so would be Tunisia or Morocco, followed by Lebanon. Countries that have immense wealth due to their oil reserves will be the last to join. However, as time passes, Middle East oil will be less and less needed in the world, and the economic welfare of oil producing countries will be at risk and this will encourage them to join.

France will play a major role in convincing the Middle East to join the Global Union. By that time the Middle East conflicts will have been solved, and once the United States joins the union all those countries that are still hesitant will do so.

Due to the mutual admiration of the Europeans and Americans, and the fact that the political and economic power in the United States lies with people whose origin is mostly from Europe, and most important because both entities share common values such as the love of freedom and democracy, all this will prevent the formation of two superpowers as in the case with the ex-Soviet Union and the United States. Instead, a union of the new superpowers will be perceived as the natural course of history.

CAN I GO ANYWHERE?

While in today's European Union any citizen of the Union can go and work in any country of the union, this might not be possible once Russia joins, or any other country that has major differences in its standard of living compared to the rest of the Union. It is no secret that access to Western Europe is restricted to citizens of Eastern Europe, because if such access were provided then Western Europe would be overwhelmed by Eastern European immigrants searching for better living conditions than those provided in their countries.

A point worth noting is that countries such as the Czech Republic or Hungary enjoy a higher standard of living than countries such as Russia or Ukraine, thus they can be integrated faster into the European Union, and their citizens can travel and work freely anywhere in the union because major immigration activities from these two countries is not expected.

I would expect a union by stages to be a wiser course to take with Russia and less fortunate Eastern European countries. Some of the obstacles for full integration reside in the level of corruption in such countries, and the formidable force that special interest groups have gained over the government and population as a whole.

However, such obstacles can be overcome and a step-by-step union strategy can be devised in a way to ultimately fully integrate Russia and the rest of Eastern Europe.

As far as India and China are concerned, full access is obviously not possible until the standard of living is raised, and the Communist system fully abandoned by the Chinese.

In recent history China has shown an ability to gradually move closer to a Capitalist system, while it maintains a centralized political command under the Communist regime, and at the same time does not admit that it is indeed moving gradually into a Capitalist system. The more the Chinese approach a democratic and capitalist system the more it becomes possible for them to get united with the rest of the world.

As far as India is concerned, its democracy and the gradual openness of its economic system will ultimately make it even closer to unification than China. However, the large populations of China and India will make it more difficult for full integration to take place.

I would imagine the ability of the union to absorb both China and India at the same time to be limited. Assuming that Russia and Eastern Europe as well as many parts of the Middle East would have already joined the union, the population of the union would still be less than the population of India alone. Thus, economic and cultural integration is needed in order to reach full integration.

While economic integration is underway, cultural integration might prove more difficult to attain. At this stage, one needs to define the term 'cultural integration.'

CULTURAL INTEGRATION

During my five-year stay in the United States I heard terms such as 'melting pot,' or 'bowl of salad' to describe the composition and relationship between different cultures that comprise American society.

I had a discussion once with an American friend about the relationship between different races. He told me that he lived in a neighborhood where there was a real sense of community and togetherness between the different races because, as he put it: "We were all poor."

Indeed, the proverb "Birds of a feather flock together" is a very interesting one. First the term *a feather* may not only mean people of the same origin or same race; it may mean people with the same level of income, occupation and education.

So, if we are talking about a world with one government and global citizens that have common sets of beliefs, we are not talking about making people lose their cultural heritage.

The term *cultural integration* has nothing to do with a process that makes the human species move towards a preconceived set of beliefs that favor one culture or another. Rather, it means communication between different cultures, which inevitably will lead each person to influence and be influenced, and thus the more people communicate the more they change.

Perhaps the most obvious example is when people get married. It is normal to expect a rocky period of integration in the first two years or so, a period when most couples go through an adjustment process where lots of fights and make-ups happen. As time goes by one would notice that the husband and wife have changed in a way that some of their opinions of each have been adopted by the other and each one acts as if these adopted opinions were their own all along.

The global citizen is a person who carries his or her cultural heritage with him or her, but not blindly: He or she is a person who believes human life is precious, and there is a feeling of respect for fellow human beings and the environment as a whole.

This does not mean that one has to socialize with people of different social classes to prove that he or she has respect for other human beings, but this means laws need to be set and implemented. Everyone is equal under the law.

This very simple fact does not exist today because, just by living in different countries, the very notion of an equitable law for the whole human species is being shattered.

In most academic books that are taught in Western cultures, the beginning of the Western civilization is traced back to the Ancient Greek civilization. I have not seen enough studies that document the effect of early civilizations brewed in China, Africa, the Middle East and other parts of the world on the Greek civilization.

THE UNIVERSAL COCKROACH

The fact that Western civilization does not properly acknowledge positive input from other civilizations is a political position that is based on arrogance.

On the other hand, other civilizations keep on stressing the value of their own civilizations, and not acknowledging the effect of Western civilization on their own, at least in the recent past.

Once the human being considers all civilizations to be an outcome of the journey of the human race on this earth, and in all civilizations a process of trial and error is continuously underway, then attitudes become more relaxed and cultures are more open to embrace each other.

Back to our main line of thought: Cultural integration is a process. It starts with putting people under one set of equitable, non-differentiating, non-biased laws and ends up by producing people who do not know what the big deal is if one has his origins in Africa or Sweden. The second part of this process has not happened yet anywhere in the world.

This does not mean that people coming from different cultures are expected to think and act in a similar way the minute they are integrated, but it means a conscious plan is to be devised so that the third and fourth generations are much more assimilated. And the plan is very simple: equitable laws, free quality education and health care, as well as acceptable living conditions.

NAWFAL MOUGHNIEH

The more unity is achieved between countries, the less distant we become from a global society with a common heritage, at the same time-sharing a common history of diversified heritage.

NATIONALISM AND DEMOCRACY

It would be beneficial at this point to explore the effects of nationalism on democracy.

Taking the classical definition of a democratic country where people elect their representatives and where power is not concentrated in one body, we discover that powerful nations can afford to be democratic because weaker nations are unable to influence or interfere with their internal politics.

So, while democracy is indeed an achievement that the West—such as the United States and Europe—ought to be proud of, it is in no way a possibility that is easily available for weak countries.

To start with, the strong countries do not let the weaker ones brew their own democracy simply because the national interest of strong countries may not coincide with the policies of the democratically elected representatives of weaker countries.

An example is what happened in South America during the Cold War period, where the United States was supporting dictators because these dictators had been perceived as strong enemies to the forces of Communism in their countries.

The United States would have loved to support democratically elected representatives that were staunch enemies of Communism in South America, but when the choice was between a dictator who was perceived as fighting Communism in his country and a democratically elected body of government (or at least a government that is supported by the majority of people) who seemed to be wishing to turn the country into a Communist regime, there is no doubt that the US would support the dictator.

This is a classical case that shows how we are all caught in a situation where we are forced to act against our convictions. The United States is forced to support dictatorship and the South American country suffers the perils of being thus governed. It may be argued that the long-term effect is beneficial to both the United States and the South American country, where the US stops the domino effect of losing so many countries to Communism, and the South American country escapes the perils of that ideology. However, the fact that we live in a world made of different countries pushes us to decide between choices of lesser evil, and not choices of better good.

Thus, putting the relation of democracy to nationalism in a more conceptual manner, we can say that under our system of multiple nations, democracy is only possible for strong nations. The system tends to encourage stronger nations to interfere in the internal affairs of weaker ones in order to make sure that the policies of weaker nations are in accordance with the national interest of the strong nations.

On a regional level as well as a global level we often find

dictators that are supported by democracies or dictators that are supported by other dictators because their interests match.

What is even more troublesome is that while nationalism and global democracy are mutually exclusive, national interest is extremely difficult if not impossible to define under a system of multiple nations.

WHAT IS THE NATIONAL INTEREST?

I cannot count the number of times I have heard the phrase 'National Interest' being uttered by government spokesmen or officials. However, it is rarely explained exactly how a certain decision or position taken by government officials is actually in the national interest of their country.

It seems to me that it is always possible to justify if a certain action is or is not in the national interest of a country. Let us take, for example, the national interest of any country where fighting terrorism is concerned.

One can argue that the best way to fight terrorism is to wage an all-out effort wherever it is located in the world. According to this argument there is an underlying assumption that no matter what the historical conditions that allowed such people to exist, the national interest is to eliminate such groups and the infrastructure that they depend on.

One can also argue that in doing so, one might end up creating new breeds of terrorists that will be far more dangerous that the ones at hand, because the more one fights different groups the more these groups have followers that are convinced that the biggest terrorists, if one can label them as such, are the countries waging the preemptive war.

It is like fighting bacteria with antibiotics: The new generation of viruses is immune to the old generation of antibiotics, and one could argue that the fact that doctors and medical researchers do not know a better way to fight bacterial infections is what makes them use the antibiotics even though they are not an ideal way to fight them.

Thus the fact that countries are unable to properly diagnose what causes certain people to use violence as a political message in the first place makes them revert to violence itself to solve the problem.

So what would the national interest of any country be to wage an all-out global war on terrorism, or to find out what the reasons or conditions are that make people violent, and try to eliminate these reasons?

All of us are caught between a rock and a hard place.

It seems to me the best way to fight terrorism is to ensure the majority of the human species feels enfranchised in an equitable global system.

GOOD FOR YOU AND FOR ME

One needs to acknowledge the fact that developed countries are largely responsible for their economic good fortunes mainly due to the hard and creative work of their citizens. Indeed, anyone who is remotely aware of the new industries being created and the tremendous hard work and creativity that has been behind the vision to build such industries can only congratulate the human species as a whole for such achievements.

Achievements in the field of information technology or biotechnology, among other fields, make one proud to be a human being.

On the other hand, one wonders if such countries can continue to exist in the same world as countries where a child is dying from hunger, or where the daily objective of the normal citizen is to find a way to have enough to eat and drink without being shot.

While it is not an acceptable argument to say that the powerful nations are to be blamed for the misfortunes of the weaker ones, one can still wonder if stability and peace can be achieved in advanced countries under such a situation.

Nietzsche said that morals were invented by the weak to

protect themselves from the strong. Forgetting about morals for the time being, would it be the national interest of countries to continue to have the world running as it is?

I say we need to formulate a vision that will put the human species as a whole under one global political umbrella.

WORLD POPULATION

Back again to the issue of world population. Two points need to be tackled: World population first, and then the increase of demographic rates on earth.

It is estimated today that the population of the earth amounts to six billion, China and India having the largest numbers.

We have talked before about an imagined scenario that would unfold for the unification of the world to take place. We have put a special emphasis on the central role of the European Union in this unification process. Today the European Union has put certain criteria for new members to be accepted.

A country that wishes to join needs to adhere to certain economic as well as social standards. A potential member needs to prove they follow certain requirements in human rights practices. These requirements have already had a positive effect on countries in Eastern Europe as well as countries along the Mediterranean that wish to join.

While so far these standards are perceived to be tailored to East European or Mediterranean countries, a time will come when the issue of enlarging the European Union to include India and China will be considered.

The sheer population size of these countries makes it extremely difficult for them to join, but on the other hand, one would argue that by the time they join, the European Union would have integrated the Middle East, Russia, and all Eastern Europe under its umbrella. Still, the Chinese and Indian governments need to work more aggressively to decrease the number of their population.

One scenario would be that massive education programs are to be devised in order to make people more aware of the consequence of having more children. While I suspect such programs would have a satisfactory effect, I would tend to imagine that advances in medicine and biotechnology would make it possible for human beings to control the number of children they have.

In order for China and India to be further encouraged to decrease their populations, I would imagine that certain incentives are to be devised by the EU; the more population is decreased the more the process of integration will be likely to take place.

Anyway, it is quite obvious even today that India and China are unable to continue living with this vast number of people.

PHILANTHROPY AND SELF INTEREST

By this stage of EU integration, it would have developed a certain ideology that distances itself more and more from its origin in Europe, and more and more encompassed the notion of the 'global human being.' By this time all civilizations and all ideas would be considered to belong to the human species, and the notion of conflict of civilizations would be replaced by the healthy competition of ideas, because civilizations would be adopting each other's views. While they could still be differentiated, violence would be gradually taken out as one of the tools of interaction.

It is this feeling of doing something of value in this world, coupled with the intelligence that concludes it is in the self-interest of the European Union to take a leadership role in uniting the world that will save the day. (Actually it will also save tomorrow, but first we need to give the EU time today to consolidate its integration process.)

ENERGY

After the world has united the global government will have to think about the energy resources that the world population needs.

Looking at energy resources today we find out that they are mostly in the hands of multinational companies and countries. I would assume that such an arrangement is not beneficial to the future world we are imagining, because such energy belongs to the world and not to a few corporations and countries.

It seems to me that sellers and producers of nonrenewable energy are to be taxed in a way to benefit the global and the regional governments, and studies need to be conducted in order to prevent monopoly of nonrenewable energy resources.

This is because the reduction in military expenses alone is not enough to finance the vast educational and healthcare needs of two-and-a-half billion people, which is assumed to be the world government's world population target. The number is not as important as the fact that a number needs to be set, and policies need to be devised and implemented in order to make sure that the level of assault on the environment is reduced to an acceptable level, while a healthy economy supporting an acceptable standard of living, is maintained.

Regional and global governments would each take a part of the revenues from the energy sold, whether they are coalmines, gas, electricity, oil, or any new energy that is not renewable.

RELIGION

As we have said before, any religion has both a unifying and a dividing role, just as the case when one creates a new country: People from within are separated from people from outside. While certain countries today have been successful in separating politics from religion, at least in their laws, it is still a difficulty to do so in other countries where religion interferes with and shapes the structure of the political set up of the society.

One interesting example is Islam, where the religion speaks about the shape of government and identifies certain aspects of economic behavior, such as preventing interest accruing to a Muslim from depositing his money in a bank.

In my opinion it is very possible to integrate various societies in the world without compromising their religious faith. For example, a Muslim can opt to deposit his money in institutions that are based on profit sharing, which is being done today already.

As for the shape of the government that Islam dictates for its followers, the principles of fair representation and equitability of an Islamic government are shared with the secular governments that exist today around the world, thus elements of similarity are far more than elements of division.

It is the Arab-Israeli conflict and the fact that most Muslim nations are living in poor conditions that have more to do with the conflict between the Islamic and the Western worlds today than differences of ideology or religion.

The Arab-Israeli conflict, or any other conflict that involves two countries, such as India and Pakistan over Kashmir, will cease to exist when we live in a world with one government, and the gap between the rich and poor is narrowed so that the root causes of violence are adequately addressed.

It is also worth noting that the budgets of local and regional governments that have specific non-contradictory tasks within the global government are partly derived from local taxes. It is beyond the scope of this essay to run these numbers.

It is very important to note that a society that adheres to the separation of state and religion is an ideal society for the thriving of religions, because it protects, under its laws, freedom of expression and worship for all, while a theocracy protects only the official religion, and in the long run might harm the very religion it wishes to protect because it turns the country into a dictatorship, against which people will ultimately revolt.

It is worth noting that any secular society has the origin of part of its laws derived from religion: as such, religious heritage plays a role in the future of mankind. The challenge is to make it play a positive role.

GLOBAL VERSUS REGIONAL AND LOCAL GOVERNMENTS

Until now we have not talked about how governmental work would be divided between the global, regional, and local governments. I would assume that it would be according to logical and practical considerations. For example, garbage collection is not something to be dealt with on a global level; rather it is something to be dealt with on a town or city level. However, environmental laws that affect garbage disposal need to be discussed at the global, regional and local levels.

Indeed, many bodies of legislation need to be thought of, on all levels, thus the executive, judicial, and legislative branches need to be devised, and the jurisdiction of governmental agencies needs to be clarified. However, the intricacies of such a matter need a collective mind so will not be discussed here.

ECONOMICS

Looking at the history of economic thought in the twentieth century, we find that although Communist thought was prevailing in many countries it failed to deliver a better life. One of the major reasons for such a failure is the fact that if everything belongs to the state, by taking property rights you are taking away the incentive for people to better themselves.

In the Capitalist countries, two schools of thought prevailed; in the middle of the twentieth century it was thought that the state needed to interfere through its fiscal policies, such as increasing or decreasing public works in order to lessen the negative effects of recession or inflation. Thus states owned a considerable part of the economy, such as the coalmines in Britain. The thinker behind such a line of thought was the economist John Maynard Keynes.

The turning point came in the 1980s with Margaret Thatcher and Ronald Reagan when they believed in less government: They believed that market forces should regulate the economy instead of the government.

Thus coalmines in Britain were privatized and the transportation industry in the United States was deregulated. The thinker behind such a line of thought was the economist Friedrich von Hayek and his student, Milton Friedman.

Let us turn our attention to envision the kind of economy that needs to prevail in our future world of one political entity.

First we need to take into consideration two periods. The first is the transitory period that lies between now and some point in the future where the global government becomes a fact, and the second is a more stable period that starts at the end of the first.

During the first period where integration is taking place but is not complete, one has to be careful not to fall into two major traps.

Since, according to our vision, free quality education and healthcare need to be given to everyone, this will automatically put a financial burden on the global government to provide such a wide social net.

It seems to me such a policy cannot be implemented in haste. To start with we do not want rich countries to fall into the trap of providing social services for other poor countries and depriving themselves of this money.

We also do not want poor countries to start selling or privatizing their state-owned companies and natural resources in order to pay for the social programs we are talking about. We certainly do not want what happened in Russia when state-owned companies that owned vast amounts of natural resources were sold dirt cheap to private investors after Communism collapsed.

THE UNIVERSAL COCKROACH

So, where would the money come from?

It has to come from the increase in the size of the poor countries' economies as these countries slowly integrate with the others. Investment, technology, and managerial know-how start flowing from developed to less developed countries, and once the economies of poorer countries become stronger and their public companies get their finances and operations in order, then it is no problem to privatize selected public companies, provided that studies are done on a case-by-case basis for each publicly-owned asset to be privatized.

This way enough money will be provided for social services and investments. As much as this scenario is possible to be realized, by just looking at the economic history of different countries, we notice that some regions or countries will definitely not be able to have their economies expand in the way we are hoping, for different reasons specific to each country and region.

In order to minimize such a possibility from happening, and taking into consideration that expert advice has already been given to such failed economies but did not work, then a special program needs to be implemented where the slowing down of integration is to take place, and a step-by-step integration is to be envisioned in order to make sure that the ills of such economies are rectified: Then the integration process can pick up speed for such countries with failed economies.

A valid question is raised now: What would be the identity of the body that would be responsible for managing the integration of the world?

It is clear that the World Bank and other international organizations failed to permanently rescue ailing economies in different countries.

The failure of such organizations is inevitable because there are two players with two different agendas; namely countries that are net producers of technology, and countries that are net consumers of technology.

The first group is interested in opening new markets and lowering trade barriers so that the exports of their value added goods can be enhanced.

The second group is interested in selling their commodities at the highest price possible, and protecting their non-competitive industries from international competition.

It is clear that such a situation will produce a win-lose situation; neither is the first group interested in buying commodities at a high price, nor is the second group interested in facilitating the destruction of ailing industries.

While it is true that foreign investments have a net positive effect on the economies of both groups, this investment is not enough to ensure a country achieves its social and economic objectives.

Back to our main question: Who will manage the integration of the whole world?

As I mentioned previously, the European Union is in the best position to do so.

It is true that the ideology of the European Union is not that of unifying the world under its umbrella, rather it is expanding the European Union to encompass what has traditionally been considered Europe.

Even Turkey can be considered traditionally part of Europe: After all, modern day Istanbul was Constantinople, and the fact that Europe has set criteria for Turkey to fulfill in order to be eligible to join, is a very positive step towards the unification process.

I would envision special commissions within the European Union that would set criteria for all regions and countries in the world, to make it possible for them to join the EU once they have been fulfilled. At some stage, as said before, the EU would change its name to be the GU, the Global Union.

It would be wise, as a cautious strategy and in the interim period before total integration takes place, to create a global entity calling itself the GU. The GU would initially encompass the EU and all countries that would join; and this way, in case set-backs happen, the EU would retain its initial European identity and be immune from such set- backs, whilst at the same time the integration process would have a tremendous boost from having the EU supporting it as one of its members. Other groups of countries can join the GU, such as Russia and the ex-Soviet Union, states that are not under the EU umbrella.

As far as the United States is concerned, I put my bets on the wisdom, intelligence, and especially diversity of the American people that will ultimately lead them to endorse the unification process. After all, a unified world encompassing all cultures and all human beings as individuals having equal rights and responsibilities under the law is only a mirror of the American society as the American majority ideally thinks it of today.

The citizens of the United States have their origins in countries all over the world; they have different backgrounds and cultures. It would be ideal for the long-term stability of the United States to live in a world that has societies that enjoy democracy and cultural diversity. This way, even if the United States did not initially join the GU, it would have a reason to support the unification process, because that would result in global citizens that are more democratic and culturally tolerant, which is an American objective.

It is very important today to note that the European Union is not perceived as conducting an imperial policy while it is integrating East Europe; this has a lot to do with the wisdom that Europe has gained through the centuries. This wisdom makes it attractive for many countries to join the Union. Granted that few European countries show signs of immaturity in their way of thinking, especially as far as international politics are concerned, it is safe to say that decisions or statements made by the EU as a whole are wise and sensible.

Indeed, if the United States and Europe throw their weight behind global unification, this will make the process much faster. It is important, however, not to force unification at any time, but rather make it an attractive process by showing the benefits for societies under unification.

I hate to leave the above paragraphs painting a rosy picture of the unification process without mentioning the possible mistakes that could happen on the way.

A case in point is what is happening today in Ukraine. In my opinion, the EU has eroded its standing greatly by not sending a clear signal of its desire to integrate Russia, Belarus, and Ukraine—all at the same time. The result of this failure is a great tension between the western citizens of Ukraine that are pro-EU and the eastern part of Ukraine that are pro-Russia.

The perception today in Russia and the eastern part of Ukraine is that the EU and the United States are dealing in a Cold War mentality with the three sisters—they wish to surround Russia with NATO forces and deprive Russia of Ukraine's economic and political space, thus choking the possibility of Russia again becoming a superpower.

Back to economics, which after all was the title for this section: The economies of different countries in the first stage, which is the transition state, will not be entirely coupled with each other or with other countries outside the Union. Indeed, the ability of different cultures and economies to seize the potential opportunities that lie in the unification process varies widely.

As time goes on, it will be possible for the transfer of technology, brains and investments to flow freely among the regions of the unified globe, thus making it possible for a homogeneous standard of living to exist all over the world. The objective of course is not only a homogeneous standard of living, but rather a continuous process of development of the human species and all species on Earth.

It is clear now that the fate of all living species on Earth depends on the actions of the human species. It is true that 99 percent of all living species had ceased to exist even before the human being became influential in forming the destinies of other species. However, due to the process of natural selection, i.e. survival of the fittest, today we are destroying the remaining one percent at an alarming rate. The way the human species is conducting its business today makes it more and more difficult for other species to adapt, including the human species itself.

It is absolutely essential to enlighten every member of the human species in order to have a positive long lasting effect on the quality of the environment as a whole. This hopefully will make people who are primarily concerned with the environment, support the unification process, and perceive it not as an attempt at hegemony in disguise, but rather as an honest attempt to make the human species as a whole more enlightened.

Thus, once the integration stage is finalized, and different economies are coupled together, then we will witness the emergence of a global society that provides equal opportunities and equal rights.

THE MOST IMPORTANT FOUNDATION FOR DEMOCRACY

I would expect the education bill for educating the global citizens of the world to be high, because the rate of education is not only calculated based on the incremental income that an educated versus uneducated person would enjoy; it is also based on the contribution of education to the general level of awareness and knowledge that the global society must possess in order for democracy to have any meaning.

What is meant by that is that one of the foundations of democracy is the ability of a society to elect *its* representatives. If the society does not have the proper knowledge to choose appropriate representatives, then it will end up harming itself.

WHAT A GLOBAL GOVERNMENT CANNOT DO?

It might be as important to explore a global government's limits of achievements, or the limits of achievements of a world with one political system.

We have briefly mentioned the fact that special interest groups will have an effect on the decisions of a global government, as they have an effect today on the decisions made by all countries-big or small, weak or strong.

I feel I need to explore this matter further, and one question comes to my mind: Whom do special interest groups represent?

A special interest group of elderly citizens might represent an important part of a society, and a special interest group of oil companies represents a minority. However, the fact that the first group represents a majority and the second group a minority does not alone justify the validity or usefulness of each group. Indeed, oil companies might have sound and legitimate concerns, at the same time they might not, this is also true for the elderly group, and this poses a new question: Who will decide the legitimacy or benefit of the agendas pushed by any group?

At the final stage, things boil down to the total education level of the citizens of the world.

Thus, as a general statement we can say that any political system cannot deliver at any moment a better quality of decision and planning process than what the collective mind of people has achieved at that moment in time. In other words, you cannot give what you do not have. Therefore, it is worth noting that global education is absolutely essential for ensuring that the level of education and knowledge in general is being continuously improved, and this will be positively reflected on the quality of the planning, decision making and execution processes.

GLOBAL NATION CONSTITUTION

Looking at the constitutions of different countries today, we find some elements in certain constitutions more advanced than others. Issues such as women's rights, individual rights, freedom of expression, respect of different cultures and philosophies or religions, and many other issues need to be addressed in order to have a constitution that takes care of different modern issues, such as protecting the environment, as well as enabling supreme courts to pass judgment with as much fairness as possible.

Drafting this constitution is one of the important foundations for our vision to be realized, and the work of drafting the constitution can start today, even before our vision is realized.

A FINAL THOUGHT

I finish this essay with one thought: The welfare of the human and other species needs collective work, and unifying the whole world as one entity is a necessary but not sufficient condition for the success of such collective work.

REFERENCES

Alexander, P. (Editor). 1982. *Lion Handbook of World's Religions.* Oxford: Lion.

Attenborough, D. 2003. *Life on Earth, The Living Planet and The Private Life of Plants.* DVD. London: BBC.

Bronowski, J. (Presenter). 2005. The Ascent Of Man. DVD. BBC.

Brook, P. 1989. *The Mahabharata.* DVD. Bfi Video Publishing.

Cain, T. 2004. *The Book of Rule: How the World Is Governed.* New York: DK Publishing

Darwin, C. 1958. *The Origin of Species: By Means of Natural Selection or the Preservation of Favoured Races in the Struggle for Life.* New York. Mentor

Guitry, S. (Director) 2001. *Napoleon: The Epic Life of a Great French Leader (1955).* DVD. Brentwood.

Jones, W.T. 1969-80. *A History of Western Philosophy.* Five Volumes. New York: Harcourt Brace Javanovich.

Kennedy, P.M. 1987. *The Rise and Fall of the Great Powers: Economic Change and*

Military Conflict from 1500 to 2000. New York : Random House.

Kissinger, H. 1994. *Diplomacy.* New York: Simon & Schuster.

Koval, M. (Director). 2003. *Empires—Peter & Paul and the Christian Revolution.* DVD. PBS Paramount.

Kuhn, T.S. 1970. *The Structure of Scientific Revolutions.* Chicago: University of Chicago Press.

Machiavelli, N. 2003. *The Prince.* London: Penguin.

O'Brien, P.K. (Editor). 2000. *Philip's Atlas of World History From the Origins of Humanity to the Year 2000.* London: George Philip.

PBS Special. 2003. *Evolution.* DVD. PBS.

Sabine, G.H. and Thorson, T.L. (Editors). *A History of Political Theory.* New York: Harcourt Brace Jovanovich.

Schama S. 2000. *A History of Britain: The Complete Series.* DVD. BBC.

Smith, H. 1996. *The power Game.* New York: Ballantine.

Stiers, D.O. (Narrator). 2002. *Commanding Heights—Battle for the World Economy: The Battle of Ideas/The Agony of Reform/The New Rules of the Game.* DVD. Wgbh Boston

Tannenbaum, E.R. (Editor). c1973. *A History of World Civilizations.* New York : Wiley

The History Channel. 2005. *The Crusades: Crescent & the Cross.* DVD. A&E Home Video

The History Channel. 2003. *Russia: Land of the Tsas.* A&E Home Video.

Viotti, P.R. and Kauppi, M.V. (Editors). 1992. *International Relations Theory: Realism, Pluralism, Globalism and Beyond.* New York: Macmillan.

Winsor Studio. 2002. *China: A Century of Revolution.* DVD. Winsor.

ABOUT THE AUTHOR

Nawfal Moughnieh has a Bachelor's Degree in Mechanical Engineering from the American University of Beirut, and a Master's in Business Administration from the University of Rhode Island in the United States. Born in the south of Lebanon, he has lived and worked in Lebanon, the United Arab Emirates, Saudi Arabia, and the United States. His world travels exposed him to different cultures and ideologies and sparked his interest in the possibility of a global union. He currently works as a business consultant for the Middle East and lives in Lebanon.